W9-CTU-750

Conducting Better Job Interviews

Second Edition ◆ Robert F. Wilson

BARRON'S

ACKNOWLEDGMENTS

A number of friends and colleagues have contributed significantly to the improvement of this edition, foremost among them Martha Buchanan; Frances Hesselbein, The Drucker Foundation; Mark Johnson, YMCA; Lisa Pandolino, Ben & Jerry's; Audrey Rothstein, College and University Personnel Association; Jill Tavello, Stew Leonard's; William Sharwell, former president, Pace University; and Tracey Topper, Barron's Educational Series, Inc.

Copyright © 1997 by Barron's Educational Series, Inc.
Prior edition © 1991 by Barron's Educational Series, Inc.

All rights reserved.

No part of this book may be reproduced in any form, by photostat, microfilm, xerography or any other means, or incorporated into any information retrieval system, electronic or mechanical, without the written permission of the copyright owner.

All inquiries should be addressed to:
Barron's Educational Series, Inc.
250 Wireless Boulevard
Hauppauge, New York 11788

Library of Congress Catalog Card No. 97-10351

International Standard Book No. 0-8120-9893-5

Library of Congress Cataloging-in-Publication Data
Wilson, Robert F.
    Conducting better job interviews / by Robert F. Wilson. — 2nd ed.
      p.   cm. — (Barron's business success series)
    Includes bibliographical references and index.
    ISBN 0-8120-9893-5
    1. Employment interviewing.   I. Title.   II. Series.
HF5549.5.I6W55   1997
658.3'1134—dc21   97-10351
                                                  CIP

PRINTED IN HONG KONG
987654321

Contents

◆

Introduction v

Chapter 1
Interviewing to Hire:
Organizational Priorities in Hiring Policy 1

Chapter 2
Interview Preparation: *Résumés, Application Forms,*
Testing, and the Screening Interview 19

Chapter 3
Conducting Selection Interviews:
Establishing a Win-Win Personal Meeting 41

Chapter 4
Evaluating the Interview:
Tools to Facilitate the Decision Making Process 55

Chapter 5
Job Offer and Compensation Negotiation:
Final Steps Leading to Hire 69

Chapter 6
Other Job-Related Interviews:
*Performance Evaluation, Voluntary and
Involuntary Termination Meetings* 77

Bibliography 91

Appendix
*Interview Guides, Sample Evaluation Sheets,
Acceptance/Rejection Letters, Permissible/Prohibited
Inquiries, Position Outline, and Job Application Forms* 93

Index 121

Introduction

◆

More hiring mistakes are made because of improper, incomplete, or inefficient interviewing than any other reason. Every year hundreds of millions of corporate dollars are wasted as a result of employees being placed in positions for which they are unsuited or turned down for jobs they are qualified to fill. More important, the professional lives that have been misused as a result of people working at jobs for which they are not suited—and of people passed over because interviewers have failed to recognize their talent—represent countless individual, yet avoidable, personal tragedies.

The purpose of this book is to cut these human and financial losses by providing managers with the tools to identify, evaluate, and attract the right people—and enrich their professional lives in the process.

Chapter 1

◆

Interviewing to Hire:

Organizational Priorities in Hiring Policy

> *"Man is so made that he can only find relaxation from one kind of labor by taking up another."*

—Anatole France

Finding and hiring the best people is a skill that few managers have. Largely this is because managers are not encouraged to develop this skill. Many CEOs and senior managers fail to recognize that interviewing and evaluating prospective employees is an integral part of a manager's job. As a consequence, in many organizations little money is spent on training interviewers to be as effective as they can be. First impression and intuition have by default become the twin gods of hiring decisions for most managers.

The long-range consequences of this oversight are great—for you, for those you interview, and for your organization.

Whether you're a line manager hiring a key specialist, or a human resource department interviewer screening candidates for an open position, you must have a well-thought-out system for making hiring decisions.

Your opinion and evaluation of job candidates should be backed by an effective review mechanism. This will decrease your chances of hiring the wrong person, and prevent good candidates from slipping through the cracks. Whether your institution hires five people a year or five thousand, the most important contribution you can make to the process is to *implement*—or, if you have the opportunity, *formulate*—a policy that is both objective and foolproof.

In this book you will see how several companies and nonprofit organizations implement policies and practices to ensure that they hire the best possible people. Even though their philosophies vary, you will see that all have developed rigorous, formalized hiring plans. Use or adapt any of their methods appropriate to your situation.

Although most of this book is devoted to the hiring process, we also will deal with other situations that involve interviewing skills. These are:

◆ Job evaluation interviews

◆ Information interviews

◆ Exit interviews

These interviewing situations are covered in Chapter 6.

CORPORATE MISSION

All recruitment and hiring decisions should be based on a single question: Is this decision consistent with our corporate or organizational mission?

Any organization—whether a for-profit corporation or a nonprofit foundation or hospital—functions best when its day-to-day activities reflect its reason for existence, or its mission. Identifying a mission leads to goal setting. Linked to goals are objectives, which in turn lead to action steps, a budget, and an appraisal process.

Although the nonprofit sector represents just 2 to 3 percent of the U.S. gross national product, management author Peter Drucker calls it "America's largest employer," insofar as every other adult spends on average three hours per week volunteering for one or more nonprofit organizations. "The non-profit institution 'product' is neither a pair of shoes nor an effective regulation," says Drucker in *Managing the Non-Profit Organization.* "Non-profit institutions are human-change agents. Their 'product' is a cured patient, a child that learns, a young man or woman grown into a self-respecting adult; a changed human life altogether."

Every organization should have a recruitment and hiring strategy designed to implement its direction and purpose. This corporate mission will change as a company changes, in response to both inside and outside influences. But at any given time a clear statement of corporate purpose should inform the hiring policy of every department and function, from executive vice president to mailroom.

One New York electronics company has charted its mission and implementation plan as follows:

The recruitment manager for this firm traces the existence of its mission statement to a question the firm's president asked her some time ago. "He asked how we knew we were hiring the right people," she says. "When we thought it through, we realized that additional tools were needed to be sure our field managers were hiring sales and support people for the right reasons."

As you can see from the diagram, all of the company's recruiting decisions flow from this grand design. The company's mission statement also has been translated to a video format, which means that every employee can internalize both short- and long-term goals.

Some for-profit corporations blur the distinction from nonprofit organizations by adding a social dimension to their mission statements. "Linked prosperity," for example, is the mission followed by Ben & Jerry's Ice Cream, of South Burlington, Vermont. This mission consists of three interrelated parts: a "product mission," which sets forth standards for the ice cream it makes and distributes; an "economic mission," which encompasses goals for profitability and growth; and a "social mission," which includes a concern for the community in day-to-day business decisions.

As partial fulfillment of Ben & Jerry's social mission, 7.5 percent of all pretax profits go to philanthropy, allocated by a foundation made up of company employees and administered through employee-led community action teams. "In addition," says Liz Bankowski, director of social mission for the company, "all employees participate in a company-sponsored recycling program—mandatory on the job and voluntary at home."

San Francisco's Levi Strauss & Company has approached its mission slightly differently. With the encouragement of president Robert Haas, employees have created an "Aspirations Statement" that articulates the values the company stands for. Every employee hired is asked to subscribe to the six "leadership tenets" described in this statement, at least two of which (Diversity and Empowerment) are very likely uncharacteristic of most corporations you may be familiar with. Here are the six leadership tenets:

◆ *New Behaviors*—directness, openness to influence, commitment to the success of others, personal accountability, teamwork, and trust.

◆ *Diversity*—a diverse workforce (age, sex, ethnic group) at all levels, diversity in experience, and diversity in perspectives. Differing points of view will be sought; diversity will be valued and honesty rewarded, not suppressed.

◆ *Recognition*—financial and professional recognition for all individuals and teams that contribute to success: those who create and innovate and those who support day-to-day business requirements.

◆ *Ethical Management Practices*—adherence to stated company standards of ethical behavior. This includes clarity about expectations and a commitment to enforce these standards through the corporation.

◆ *Communications*—clarity about goals and performance for company, unit, and individual; timely, honest feedback about performance and career aspirations.

◆ *Empowerment*—a steady increase in the authority and responsibility of those closest to products and customers. An active fostering of responsibility, trust, and recognition in the organization, in a way that allows full utilization of the capabilities of all employees.

William G. Sharwell can speak to both for-profit and nonprofit area concerns. In 12 years he rose to senior vice president of AT&T, after which he resigned to accept the presidency of Pace University in New York City—a job he held for six years. Sharwell believes that the gap has closed in the way organizations in these two sectors execute their missions.

"Go back 25 years and most nonprofit organizations were kind of sleepy and slapdash," says Sharwell, "but today those of any consequence have to be as efficient and effective as a for-profit business. So I would want to make sure that anybody I hire or promote understands that and is not offended by it."

As part of its commitment to grow and nuture qualified leaders on a continuing basis, Pratt & Whitney, a division of United Technologies Corporation, selects nine recent graduates of top business schools each year as "leadership associates" for a two-year fast-track assignment. Candidates for this program are screened as rigorously as are other full-time permanent employees.

Leadership associates are given a series of six- to nine-month assignments in different areas and divisions of the company. Candidates are judged on the basis of leadership potential, intellect, personal attributes, and interpersonal and communication skills.

At the end of two years, the nine associates and management together decide the long-term future for the associates, and where the best opportunity lies for each.

The Candidate Evaluation Sheet for one successful leadership associate—along with one of the interviewer's comments and rankings—appears on page 100 of the Appendix.

JOB DESCRIPTION

Every hiring decision begins with a job description that reflects the organization's short-term and long-term needs.

Following are the basic components of a job description:

◆ Job title

◆ Job summary

◆ Description of duties and responsibilities

◆ Standards of performance against which duties and responsibilities will be measured (including, where applicable, "critical performance factors" that pinpoint optimum qualification levels)

◆ A delineation of the relationships between the job described and other jobs that impact upon it—both inside and outside the company

Analyze every job description to be sure that incompatible functions are eliminated. For example, should a busy customer service representative be required to take extensive phone orders? Should a quality control supervisor be responsible for vendor selection? Your company's structure may make a clearly defined set of responsibilities impossible, but this is a goal worth working toward.

Managers new to writing job descriptions often tend to make unrealistic demands. For example, a line manager for an electronics firm looking to fill a sales position may say she wants somebody who is actively involved in sales, who knows computer products, and who has worked in the target industry. It is essential to focus on the ideal candidate's minimally acceptable characteristics. Using the example above, is someone with quantifiable sales experience really needed, or would a trainable individual with basic selling aptitude do? If the second option is acceptable, the position's starting salary level can be reduced by perhaps $10,000 or more.

Stew Leonard's ("The World's Largest Dairy Store") of Norwalk, Connecticut, cares less about measurable skills, which it teaches on the job, than about what Jill Tavello, the company's vice president of human resources, calls "the three A's": Attitude, Approach, and Appearance. The company promotes from within almost exclusively. It concentrates on attracting entry-level people who are service oriented and who have the skills and interests that will enable them to move easily into positions of increasing responsibility. (See Appendix pages 112–119 for Stew Leonard's application form.) For example, Chris Arnette, Stew Leonard's recruiting manager, was hired as a cashier 19 years ago.

EQUAL EMPLOYMENT OPPORTUNITIES

Because of widespread discriminatory hiring practices in the past, there are now laws at the federal, state, and municipal levels that protect workers from intentional and unintentional employer bias.

The cost of employment discrimination, if such legislation did not exist, is stated forcefully as part of the introduction to the Equal Opportunities Ordinance of New Haven, Connecticut:

> "... *Discrimination and its consequences cost the city and its people dearly. They cause unsafe and unsanitary housing, unemployment, underemployment, and human waste. They also cause increased crime, juvenile delinquency, disease, fire, public disorder, deficiencies in the city's education system, higher welfare costs, and loss of tax revenue.*"

To be sure, laws of this type have not eradicated discriminatory hiring practices, but they are making an impact. It is unlawful, for example, to:

◆ Refuse to consider for employment any person because of race, color, national origin, sex, religion, age, handicap or covered veteran status, or physical disability.

- Categorize job candidates on the basis of race, color, national origin, sex, religion, or age.

- Exhibit bias in employment advertising based on race, color, national origin, sex, religion, or age—unless such considerations are legitimate requirements for performing the job competently.

- Use any screening techniques (questionnaires and tests, for example) that are not directly job related.

The consequences of violating EEO regulations at any level are severe. Stiff fines are assessed organizations that flout these ordinances—especially repeat offenders. For example, one large law firm was recently barred from recruiting at the University of Chicago for one year following a black law student's complaint that racist questions had been asked of her while she was interviewing for a position with the firm.

Individuals who believe they have been discriminated against during any recruitment process have 300 days to file a complaint. Even suspected EEO violations can be extremely time-consuming for the recruiting company, requiring the retrieval of all recruitment records and the completion of detailed statistical analyses of every applicant recruited.

The key phrase as regards violations of EEO regulations is "bona fide occupational qualification." Do your interview questions relate solely to potential performance on the job? If you can answer yes in every instance, you probably will not run afoul of EEO regulations. (See Appendix page 109 for NatWest Bank N.A.'s list of permissible and prohibited questions.)

Keep in mind that state discrimination laws usually are more stringent than federal laws. And when two laws apply, chances are you'll be held legally accountable for the more exacting of the two.

Questions about pending criminal indictments may well be relevant to job performance. For example, a person pursuing his or her defense in a legal proceeding may require substantial time off from the job. Consequently, the prospective employer is within its legal rights to postpone a hiring decision until the person is cleared of the charge. In gray areas, common sense may also be on your side. For example, a federal court recently ruled that an employer had sufficient grounds for rejecting an applicant who had been convicted of stealing a government check from the mail, because the open position was in the company's mailroom.

A much more positive way to view EEO regulations is to consider ways certain applicants might be utilized by your company rather than how to avoid penalties for not hiring them. The unemployment rate for blind or visually impaired workers, to take one example, runs at about 70 percent. Recent technology has made it much easier, though, for sightless people to be productive employees in a wide range of fields.

Today, the visually impaired have far greater access to printed documents and other data than ever before. Julia Anderson reports in the *Harvard Business Review* that "machines can read a printed page out loud, using synthetic speech, or receive typed input and produce braille output; devices, when attached to a computer terminal, will speak whatever material appears on screen; and systems can read written matter onto a disk, then output it in braille, synthetic speech, or large print."

The biggest obstacle sight-impaired workers face, says Anderson, is the bias against them by coworkers or managers who may feel uncomfortable in their presence. A short training program and a minor investment in certain equipment can eliminate this problem and help countless sight-impaired individuals become productive and valued employees. Slight adjustments in workplace equipment and attitudes can accommodate workers with other kinds of handicaps as well.

RECRUITMENT

The range of alternatives for seeking out the right people includes:

◆ internal recruitment

◆ college recruitment

◆ executive-search firms

◆ employment agencies

◆ newspaper and trade magazine advertising

◆ job fairs

◆ networking

◆ computer-aided recruitment

The computer-aided recruitment option may be new to you, but it is becoming an increasingly popular and effective tool. *HR* (Human Resources) *Magazine* keeps track of new developments in this area as they emerge, so to do the same you need to: 1) subscribe; 2) glance through a library copy of each issue; or 3) utilize one or more of the available database services, such as Infotrack or ProQuest. In addition to this, the following URL addresses should be helpful—and are also linked to additional related sources:

CareerWEB (http://www.cweb.com)
Cool Career Sites (http://www.infoseek.com/doc/netdir/career.html)

Each of these options deserves consideration before you establish recruitment policy, although in the final analysis, budget limitations may be the most critical factor in your final decision. In any case, you should realize that there are a range of options. Books that may help you prioritize your recruitment alternatives are listed in the Bibliography on page 91.

TESTING

Many companies depend to varying degrees on the formal testing and measurement of intelligence, aptitude, interest, proficiency, and temperament as aids in their hiring decisions. One company that values the testing component highly is NatWest Bank N.A. Greg D'Archangelis, assistant vice president of human resources, has overseen the establishment of a testing program for the hiring of tellers in NatWest's 130-plus-branch New York metropolitan area.

"Honesty and integrity weigh very heavily in hiring tellers," says D'Archangelis. "Testing allows us to identify individuals likely to respond well in these two areas—as well as those who may not.

"In the two years since we started the program, our turnover rate has dropped from 38 percent to 28 percent. I attribute a significant part of this to our testing."

SUBJECTIVE HIRING CRITERIA

Some companies adhere to extremely demanding or unorthodox hiring standards. North American Tool & Die president Tom Melohn believes the strict hiring standards at his firm is the biggest reason staff turnover has dropped from 27 percent to 4 percent. Melohn takes a personal hand in an exhaustive hiring process that yields just two employees out of every 300 candidates. Here are some ways he recruits employees:

◆ Placing ads in neighborhood newspapers only. (Employees with long commutes will continue to look for shorter ones.)

◆ Designing ads that will be noticed. (Two column-inches will be missed. Melohn places want ads at the top of a listing, and runs them for ten straight days.)

◆ Never hiring a person who has spent less than a year with any one employer. (You may be wrong, Melohn admits, but you eliminate every job hopper for whatever reason.)

◆ Asking for a short letter telling how the candidate fits the job, rather than a résumé. (Melohn believes this approach provides more insight into the values and communications skills of prospective employees.)

Outside Consultants

Most of you, particularly those in smaller companies or in a startup situation, will benefit occasionally from the services of an outside human resources consultant to surmount an unfamiliar challenge.

Jeff Krug, who heads J.L. Krug & Associates in Geneva, Illinois, assists human resource departments of client companies in evaluating employees being appraised for promotion or assignment change. He also tests and measures outside candidates under consideration for hire. "In today's environment," says Krug, "companies need a way to acquire enough accurate information from candidates to be sure they select only the best. Most newer managers—especially those in smaller companies—are not trained sufficiently in the hiring process to choose the best people.

"There are hundreds of preemployment assessment tools out there. Companies need to be sure that any instrument they use is both valid and a work-related one—either from a skills assessment or actual job-fit perspective. With appropriate preemployment tools we can also assess integrity, reliability, work ethic, and, in many instances, even substance abuse."

The payoff, according to Krug, is that employers using adequate preemployment assessment save themselves countless dollars and gain productivity by hiring the right people in the first place rather than training and probably firing the original hires, and going through the entire process yet again.

Chapter 2

Interview Preparation:

*Résumés, Application Forms, Testing,
and the Screening Interview*

"If a little knowledge is dangerous, where is the man who has so much as to be out of danger?"

—Thomas H. Huxley

The hiring process can be broken down into five parts, although some organizations combine them in various ways, depending upon policy or preference. The five parts are:

1. Application form and résumé review

2. Skill, intelligence, or aptitude testing

3. Screening interview

4. Selection interview

5. Offer interview

The first three parts of the hiring process are covered in this chapter. The selection interview is covered in Chapter 3. The offer interview is discussed in Chapter 5.

APPLICATION FORMS AND RÉSUMÉS

Many organizations use application forms for nonexempt[1] positions only, although some organizations have them on file for all

---

[1] The distinction between exempt and nonexempt personnel has roots in wage and hourly labor legislation dating back to the 1930s. By definitions established in this legislation, "exempt" employees include all executives, and most upper-level managers and professionals. As such, they are *exempt* from this legislation. "Nonexempt" employees, comprised largely of hourly workers, are therefore *subject* to this legislation.

employees. An application form should provide space for the applicant's educational background, work history (including employers, positions held, inclusive dates, salary, responsibilities, and reasons for leaving), and any special considerations occasioned by the nature of your company. Be sure that no request for information on your application form violates EEO regulations.

Preparation for a hiring interview should start with a comparison of the candidate's résumé and completed application form. Any inconsistencies between the two documents can be dealt with immediately and quickly.

A candidate whose résumé is not strong but who perhaps has written a compelling letter indicating an awareness of your company's problems—as well as possible solutions—is certainly worth ten to fifteen minutes of your time. Similarly, an applicant recommended highly by a colleague you respect also deserves a hearing.

Tom Melohn, president of North American Tool & Die, rejects 90 percent of all applicants after reviewing their application forms. Here are some of the factors he considers:

◆ *Is it neat?* Neatness counts, especially if you are hiring someone for a highly technical job. "Neatness indicates a caring person," says Melohn.

◆ *Is it complete?* If not, it's an indication that the person doesn't follow instructions well.

◆ *Outside interests?* Coaching soccer or singing in a choir, for example, indicates a giver, a belonger. A person who lists no personal interests—or thinks such information is nobody's business—is most likely the wrong kind of person, Melohn believes.

◆ *Relevant experience.* Skills can be taught, but only to some people. Those afraid of machines or driven mad by the thump of a punch press probably don't have the right temperament for work in a tool and die plant, Melohn feels.

Financial recruiter Robert Half advises corporate representatives who evaluate résumés to read between the lines. For example:

1. *Be wary of the functional résumé.* A functional résumé does not match dates to specific jobs; it emphasizes generic skills and accomplishments. The candidate who writes such a résumé could well be right for the job. Nevertheless, functional résumés are often written by candidates who have been job jumpers, or out of work for long periods of time.

2. *Look for profit-mindedness.* See if you can sense from the résumé whether the applicant appreciates that companies are in business to make money. For example, does the résumé include accomplishments that have helped increase earnings or saved company dollars?

3. *Watch out for trivia.* A résumé puffed up with sports interests, hobbies, and other incidental information may indicate that the

applicant is weak in experience and skills. It could also mean that the candidate won't have enough time for the job. (Note the distinction between this advice regarding résumés, which are generated by the writer, and Thomas Melohn's advice about application forms, which require an applicant's direct response to specific questions.)

4. *Don't excuse sloppiness.* An applicant who doesn't care enough to make a résumé letter perfect is not a good bet to be conscientious on the job.

Other things to look for: quantifiable accomplishments, as well as duties and responsibilities; evidences of a shaky career path, such as lateral moves, short job tenures, and multiple career changes.

Be leery of credit taken for departmental or company successes that rightfully should be shared with others. Make a note to ask what *specific* decisions the applicant made, with whom he or she worked on a given project, and what special knowledge was put into play.

INTERVIEWER PREPARATION

A number of management consulting firms provide coaching to interviewers new to the activity. Drake Beam Morin, a large outplacement company, offers a two-day workshop for entry-level human resource professionals. The purpose of the program is to assist recruiters in the selection of personnel for nonexempt, technical, and manufacturing positions. DBM offers the workshop for a fee, on demand, in all of its offices.

"Participants have responded enthusiastically to this program because of the no-nonsense, easy-to-understand, and eminently practical format and content," says Bob Graham, former general manager of DBM's Stamford, Connecticut, office.

Pratt & Whitney, one of a number of companies that provide in-house assistance for new interviewers, uses a team approach when selecting executives. The team meets beforehand to review the candidates nominated for a job opening and selects those to be interviewed. The team leader (usually the hiring executive) explains the process to the other team members. All first-time interviewers attend a one-on-one planning session with a lead interviewer and sit in on a number of live interviews before conducting one of their own. The group decides which aspects of the interview will be handled by each member.

Greg D'Archangelis of NatWest Bank N.A. has conducted 14 training sessions for branch managers and assistants. Trainees are paired off in "mock interviews" until comfortable with the techniques. Those who caught on less quickly underwent remedial training.

"We found," says D'Archangelis, "that a number of branch managers were approaching a danger zone with some of their questions. For example, some were asking female applicants about their expectations regarding child care. After this training, the managers were able to focus exclusively on job-related questions."

Human resources consultant Erik Rambusch, of Norwalk, Connecticut, has developed a sales manager's interview guide for a Dun & Bradstreet company. The guide is geared to specific success criteria, but offers enough flexibility to inform the selection of top sales candidates. Rambusch organized the guide so that it illuminates such areas as work experience, administrative ability, and sales qualities, as well as a few intangibles: attitude, willingness to accept responsibility, and management potential, among others. (The complete interview guide appears on pages 94–99 of the Appendix.)

"Most successful salespeople," says Rambusch, "move up to bigger-ticket products, larger territories, or the supervision of other sales reps. What we did in this guide was create an interview that ensured the hire of candidates with the same characteristics as today's best performers on the job."

INTERVIEW STYLES
There is a widely held belief that interview styles are a matter of preference—like choosing an entrée from a dinner menu. For example, much is made of the advantages of the "stress interview," during which interviewees are kept off balance and induced to reveal aspects of their personality or performance that would not have surfaced otherwise.

One Wall Street investment bank evaluates candidates in overheated rooms, to test their reactions to less-than-homey conditions. Other companies rely on "good cop–bad cop" adversarial confrontations, or conduct interviews using furniture that assures the interviewer of a slight height or comfort advantage over the unfortunate visitor.

Granted, such interviewing tactics may weed out applicants unable to act coolly and effectively under pressure. But there are less offensive ways to detect character traits in job applicants. For example, the kind of interview questions asked may elicit such information. Here are a few:

◆ Situational questions—create real-life hypotheses.

◆ Nondirective questions—assure nonjudgmental, open-ended give and take.

◆ Technical questions—confine emphasis to skills and technical background.

◆ Directive questions—determine candidates' values and decision making skill levels.

Most screening interviews are conducted by human resource personnel who have been briefed on the job description and any special qualifications the position requires. Candidates who survive the screening are then interviewed in greater depth by those to whom the applicant would report on the job.

Jill Tavello, vice president of human resources at Stew Leonard's, involves the human resource department receptionist in screenings. She has found that some applicants behave toward the receptionist and the interviewer in markedly different ways. Most applicants who are rude or condescending to the receptionist do not survive the screening. "For a company as driven by customer service as ours," Ms. Tavello says, "consistently courteous behavior is a must. This is a great time-saver."[1]

STRUCTURING THE INTERVIEW

Of course, interviews vary depending on the position and level being filled. However, you should always concentrate on a few specific areas to be sure you hire a person who is not only right for the job, but is right for the organization and has the capacity to grow.

CJA Career Services, in its publication *Staffing: The Bottom Line,* lists five criteria for evaluating a job applicant. Paraphrased for our purposes, they are the following:

◆ Value system
  — A strong work ethic, integrity, a sense of responsibility, principles, and a positive attitude.

---

[1] The company's customer service image received a severe blow in 1993 when Chairman Stew Leonard, Sr. was convicted and imprisoned for tax fraud, as well as for skimming $17 million from the store's daily receipts over a ten-year period. After a slight drop in sales, however, customer loyalty returned to near normal within a year.

◆ Self-esteem
— Ease in speaking about accomplishments and shortcomings, ease in giving and receiving compliments, an ability to handle criticism, a willingness to acknowledge mistakes, and an introspective nature.

◆ Intelligence
— A high intellect level, persuasiveness, an ability to be discriminating, a facility for both micro and macro thinking, a probing approach to problem solving, and inquisitiveness.

◆ Initiative
— Assertiveness, motivation, enthusiasm, and a high level of initiative.

◆ Style
— Decide which of the four basic style groups (type A/type B behaviors; theory X/theory Y management styles) are appropriate to the position, and be willing to qualify candidates according to type, such as:
— director-dominance
— politician-interactive
— diplomat-compliant
— analyzer-evaluator.

At Pratt & Whitney, the key evaluation categories are the following:

◆ Achievement—attainment of established objectives on schedule, and whether they have been exceeded; follow-through and persistence despite obstacles in pursuit of the goal.

◆ Managing Change—developing and implementing decisions that respond to or bring about change; timely, logical execution of decisions; calculated risk taking; decisiveness.

◆ Leading by Example—adhering to business and personal principles and performance standards, their accountability, how they relate to the development of trust, and leadership across normal functional boundaries.

◆ Creating a Shared Vision—perception of business issues and their integration into a vision; the communication of this vision to the organization.

◆ Building Constructive Relationships—business relationships (including staff selection, assignment, and delegation), respect for others, and communication skills.

◆ Technical Competence—the acquisition of knowledge, the processing of such knowledge, and its application to business opportunities and problems. The Pratt & Whitney Executive Selection Process *Summary Rating Form* and two of the key evaluation categories follow.

PRATT & WHITNEY EXECUTIVE SELECTION PROCESS—SUMMARY RATING FORM

POSITION _____ CANDIDATE _____

SUCCESS CHARACTERISTICS

OBSERVER	1	2	3	4	5	6	total	average
ACHIEVEMENT								
MANAGING CHANGE								
Decisiveness								
Risk Taker								
Innovative								
LEADING BY EXAMPLE								
Principled								
High Performance Standards								
Team Leadership								
CREATING A SHARED VISION								
Perceptiveness								
Business Vision								
Conceptual								
BUILDING CONSTRUCTIVE RELATIONSHIPS								
Respect for People								
Judge of People								
Communication								
TECHNICAL COMPETENCE								
Learning Orientation								
Reasoning								
OTHER FACTORS								

MANAGING CHANGE

Managing Change—relates to developing and implementing decisions and activities that respond to or bring about changes; timely, logical execution of decisions, the combination of concepts in innovative ways, and calculated risk taking.

INTERVIEW QUESTIONS

— Provide examples of key business decisions that you have made in your career.

  What were the factors leading to the decision, the causes and effects, the information available, the timing, and what was learned?

— Give examples of innovative approaches you have used to accomplish work tasks.

— What are some of the most striking examples of business risk taking that you have engaged in?

  What were the key factors in the situation, the process used to assess risk, the specific actions taken, the outcomes, and the lessons learned from the experience?

OTHER OBSERVATION METHODS

— Solicit business plans from the candidate and review them for evidence of judgment and planned results.

— Review résumé for examples of technical, organizational, or personal innovation.

— Ask the candidate's manager for examples of risk taking (either explicit or implicit) by candidate in business plans, descriptions of business results, or work.

LEADING BY EXAMPLE

Leading By Example—relates to business and personal principles and performance standards, their accountability, how they relate to the development of trust, and leadership across normal functional boundaries.

INTERVIEW QUESTIONS

— Describe your personal guiding principles as a manager.

— Give examples of specific goals you have set for yourself, another individual, or groups (business and personal).

— Describe the most challenging team leadership situation you have experienced and how you handled it.

OTHER OBSERVATION METHODS

— Solicit information from manager on specific events where candidate took positions on issues based on merit over what is politically expedient.

— In discussions with manager, customers, or peers, listen for spontaneous reference to levels of achievement, reference to the candidate being outstanding, achieving results better, faster, at lower costs than competitors, or evidencing taking positions, backing up direct reports, or accepting responsibility when things did not go well.

— Review résumé for past leadership assignments including outside leadership roles, leadership awards/recognition, assignments on special committees, experience in a matrix organization, or project management experience.

COMMON INTERVIEWING MISTAKES

In its *Interview Guide for Supervisors*,[1] the College and University Personnel Association has compiled laws and regulations governing employment practices at both state and federal levels, as well as a discussion of various aspects of the employment selection process.

Included in this useful booklet is a table of "Obstacles to Effective Interviewing," a listing of 15 common interviewing mistakes, along with probable consequences resulting from such blunders. Among them are "Failing to establish rapport with the candidate," "Asking questions answerable by a simple yes or no," and "Not listening enough." The complete table follows.

◆

OBSTACLES TO EFFECTIVE INTERVIEWING

Unfortunately, it is easy for an interviewer to make a mistake in an employment interview. Some of the common mistakes in poorly conducted interviews are as follows:

Mistakes	Comments
Failing to establish rapport with the applicant.	As a result, the interview never gets off the ground.
Not knowing what information is needed.	Consequently, the interviewer does not know whet questions to ask the applicant.

---

[1]*The Interview Guide for Supervisors* (Fourth Edition) is available from CUPA Publications, 1233 20th St., NW, Suite 301, Washington, DC 20036. Call (202) 429-0311 for price information.

Mistakes	Comments
Concentrating exclusively on the applicant as a person.	The perceptive interviewer specifically attempts to compare an applicant's demonstrated abilities and experience with the actual job requirements.
Not remaining silent, or listening, long enough.	The interviewer does too much talking and fails to obtain meaningful information from the applicant.
Not allowing sufficient time to observe the applicant's responses and behavior.	The interview should not be too short and superficial. The longer the interview, the better the chances of gaining meaningful information from the applicant.
Incorrectly interpreting information obtained from the applicant.	The interviewer draws the wrong conclusion about the applicant's ability to perform.
Being unaware of or not dealing directly with biases for or against certain types of applicants (stereotyping).	This includes how you feel about hair styles, clothing, educational background, etc. ("I have never hired a good secretary from that business college.")
Being overly influenced (either favorably or unfavorably) by one characteristic or trait of that particular applicant.	This includes physical appearances, style or dress, personality, etc. ("I can't stand men who have mustaches," or "I'd hire her for this job no matter what her previous experience.")

Mistakes	Comments
Making a decision based only on intuition or "first impression," rather than on careful insight and analytical judgment.	
Using stress techniques designed to trap or fluster the applicant.	
Conducting a poorly structured or an unstructured interview.	
Looking to see how an applicant's past life compares with the interviewer's.	This results in substantial loss of time, because more effort is spent on the "halo effect" comparison than on obtaining information relevant to the job.
Failing to control or direct the interview.	Whether out of a desire to be courteous or because the applicant is particularly dominant, the interviewer can lose control of an interview. The interviewer must regain control skillfully—not abruptly.
Asking questions answerable by a simple "yes" or "no."	People do this because their daily business conversations are often short, but in interviewing, the interviewer must endeavor to do just the opposite—draw the candidate out. This requires minimizing "yes" and "no" answers by asking open-ended questions.

Mistakes	Comments
Making judgmental or leading statements.	These telegraph to the candidate desired responses. Applicants cants can read the interviewer's mind without direct guidance.

Interviewing By Computer

Much of the rationale for computer-aided interviewing centers on countering human error, both of omission and commission. This interviewing strategy provides a base of information that can be used before the interviewer meets the applicant, and thus neutralizes, it is hoped, any overdependence on first impressions in the hiring process. It also helps to preclude the asking of illegal questions.

However, it is difficult to conceive of any computer-aided interviewing that doesn't also lead to less-than-rigorous training of interviewers. Interviewers who don't utilize their listening and observation skills to the utmost probably won't develop them fully or adequately.

Nevertheless, computer software programs can structure interviews so that questions asked of one applicant are asked of all applicants, and so that the same evaluation system is applied uniformly to each applicant. A computer software package called ProSelect, for example, provides a way to standardize the hiring process to, as its producer says, "choose a president of a company or a general laborer; a single person or dozens." ProSelect offers an "interview guide menu," from which are available a number of interview guides.

Uncovering Deception

As important as the foregoing topics are, if you aren't getting honest answers to your carefully prepared questions, you risk hiring the wrong people. Anyone hoping to become an effective interviewer must learn the dynamics of verbal and nonverbal communication, so that dishonest applicants can be easily spotted.

Dennis M. Kowal, a U.S. Army Intelligence psychologist at Fort Belvoir, Virginia, reports in *Personnel Journal* that 80 percent of communication is nonverbal rather than verbal, and that 80 percent of *that* communication is manifest in a person's face—particularly the eyes. An interviewer should be able to recognize the subtle nonverbal cues that indicate an attempt to deceive. Few applicants can lie without feeling tightness in the stomach, some involuntary change in facial expression, or diverting of the eyes from the interviewer.

Verbal cues that indicate deception include remarks as "To tell the truth," "To be perfectly honest," or "I wouldn't tell most people this." Sometimes verbal and nonverbal cues are combined—for example, an "Honest to God" remark, accompanied by a major break in eye contact, shift in body orientation, or movement of a hand to the face.

Kowal recommends a questioning strategy that increases the amount of valid, accurate information the interviewer obtains. This strategy includes several steps:

Develop rapport. An applicant will risk involvement and self-disclosure more readily when the interviewer demonstrates a genuine respect for the person and an understanding of his or her needs.

Establish congruence. Sharing anecdotes or comments during the conversation—references to previous working relationships, for example—and discussing facts and experiences that can be obtained only through experiences in the field, builds credibility. Such openness lays the groundwork for mutual sharing and honest self-disclosure on the part of the applicant.

Demonstrate acceptance. Show acceptance, interest, and respect for the applicant by being prompt, attentive, and free from distraction during the interview. Review the purpose and format for the discussion. Acknowledge questions using the applicant's choice of terms and phrases.

Pace and lead. Pinpoint hidden norms, concerns, and experiences. Elicit information to assist in understanding the interviewee's emotional state, defensiveness, and resistance. These factors reveal which mental barriers must be overcome if honest information is to be collected.

Reframe the conversation. If doubts or resistance surface, isolate them by reframing them as exceptions rather than expectations. For example, say, "I see, what you mean is that . . ." or "I realize this wasn't your intention, but you were trapped by the situation."

Acknowledge doubts as assets and the reported behaviors as reasonable under the circumstances.

Elicit honesty. Create an expectancy of honesty, a mind-set that leads to the interviewee's virtual inability to violate it. This makes the anxiety associated with admitting wrongdoing much like the anxiety associated with lying to someone who is loved and respected—for example, a parent. It is amazing what people will disclose about themselves—even at the risk of losing a job—with such subtle reframing.

Catch the pathological liar. Almost all liars are betrayed by their behavior, but most people are not skilled in recognizing this behavior. Pathological liars use certain tricks to try to convince others that they are trustworthy. They typically overstate, overreact, and overdo.

People expect a liar to be evasive and dodge difficult issues. Accomplished pathological liars know this, so they avoid such behavior. They've learned not to avert their eyes or turn away from an accuser. In fact, they seem to be too controlled, and they actually sustain eye contact far longer than is appropriate.

Lying is usually accompanied by incongruous facial responses or gestures. Note carefully the applicant's face, nose, speech, and body movements. Fragmented sentences, gestures, and slips of the tongue are also signals that the applicant may be lying. If everything else about the candidate is positive and no other interviewer shares your concerns, be sure your reference checks (see Chapter 4) are thorough in addressing these doubts before you make a final decision about the candidate.

Chapter 3

Conducting
Selection
Interviews:

Establishing a Win-Win Personal Meeting

*"A great many people think they are thinking
when they are merely rearranging their
prejudices."*

—William James

INTERVIEW QUESTIONS

The specific questions you ask during an interview, of course, vary with the position being filled and the company's hiring policy and philosophy.

Drake Beam Morin counsels in its workshops that managers get answers to three fundamental questions in any hiring interview:

1. Can the applicant do the job or be trained to do it in a reasonable period of time? "Can do" factors include abilities and basic competency requirements such as education level, job experience, knowledge, skills, and energy level.

2. Will the applicant do the job and continue to do it at the level of excellence required? "Will do" factors include motivation, incentive, drive, aspirations, goals, and interests.

3. How will the person fit in with the boss, peers, and subordinates? "How fit" factors include communications and interpersonal skills, and personal style.

NatWest N.A. has worked out a comprehensive selection interview outline for branch managers that covers a range of topics thoroughly and sequentially. The six-point outline looks like this:

1. Establish rapport
   — Greetings and introductions
   — Brief small talk

2. Set the stage
   — Why? (purpose of interview)
   — What? (what will be covered)
   — How? (sequence of events)

3. The interview: Probe using open-ended questions, and the Interview and Selection Guide.
   A. Discuss work experience: Begin with earliest jobs and proceed to most recent position
      Briefly discuss:
      — Duties and responsibilities
      — Skills and abilities
      — Public contact and service
      — Likes and dislikes
      — Difficult situations
      — Performance/attendance record
      — Reason for leaving (probe deeply for data)

B. Education and outside experiences:
- — Grade average
- — Best and worst courses
- — Extracurricular activities
- — Team involvement and other outside experiences

Note: Most of this work and education information will be on the résumé or the application. Do not have the applicant repeat information you already have.

4. Discuss and evaluate key selection criteria
- — Customer-service orientation
- — Honesty and integrity
- — Learning potential
- — Comfort with pressure
- — Team approach
- — Facility with details
- — Reliability and dependability

5. Tell and sell
- — Bank and branch structure
- — Typical daily job duties
- — Branch relationships
- — Applicant's questions and comments

6. Close interview
- — Tell applicant next step (for example, recruiter will be in contact within specified time frame). Thank applicant for coming.

An applicant able to describe his or her background in terms of the open position will help you sharpen the focus of the interview. For this reason it is a good idea to fully describe the company, the job, and qualities the successful candidate will have before asking specific, job-related questions. This may significantly increase the percentage of relevant answers you receive. The negative side of this strategy is that you may elicit some answers only because the applicant thinks you want to hear them. A probing follow-up question or two, however, usually neutralizes such self-serving responses.

BEGINNING THE INTERVIEW

Use the remaining material in this chapter as a general guideline for your hiring process.

◆ Welcome the candidate warmly. An interviewee who is at ease will be more likely to answer questions spontaneously.

◆ Introduce yourself by name and title.

◆ Ask the applicant his or her preferred name and use it throughout the interview.

◆ Sustain a relaxed atmosphere by initiating a brief conversation unrelated to the interview.

◆ Maintain an attitude of interest that will build rapport and ensure a free flow of information throughout the interview.

◆ Indicate your intention to take notes or complete your evaluation form. Invite the applicant to take notes as well, if he or she wishes to.

◆ Focus your attention fully on the applicant's responses to your questions, his or her questions and observations, and any accompanying body language.

Table 1
Key Success Characteristics for United Technologies Executives

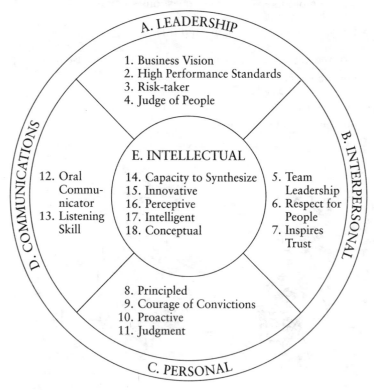

A. LEADERSHIP

1. Business Vision
2. High Performance Standards
3. Risk-taker
4. Judge of People

E. INTELLECTUAL

12. Oral Communicator
13. Listening Skill

14. Capacity to Synthesize
15. Innovative
16. Perceptive
17. Intelligent
18. Conceptual

5. Team Leadership
6. Respect for People
7. Inspires Trust

D. COMMUNICATIONS

B. INTERPERSONAL

8. Principled
9. Courage of Convictions
10. Proactive
11. Judgment

C. PERSONAL

◆ Give the applicant your complete attention, focusing fully on answers to your questions, unsolicited questions and observations, and body language.

United Technologies Corporation, in Hartford, CT, uses a rigorous executive selection procedure that allows for examination of 18 "key success characteristics" in five categories. (See Table 1.) Interviewers are asked to use at least two success characteristics for each category in every candidate assessment, or a minimum of ten characteristics per candidate. From a "tool kit" of four evidence gathering methods, evaluators must select at least three. These are:

◆ Interview

◆ Observe (for internal promotion situations only)

◆ Résumé

◆ Reference check

Each of these methods has a number of interviewing criteria that differ with the success characteristic under scrutiny. For example, under the success characteristic "high performance standards," the interviewing questions may be:

♦ Describe the approach you use to set work goals for others.

♦ Give examples of specific goals you have set:
— for an individual
— for groups

♦ Describe the approach you use to set work goals for yourself.

♦ Give examples of specific goals you have set for yourself:
— business
— personal

♦ Describe a situation in which a goal you set was not met:
— for an individual
— for a group
— for yourself

How did you handle each of these situations?

Questions such as these help a recruiter properly evaluate an interviewee who seeks to make a favorable impression based on style rather than substance. (See pages 102–103 of the Appendix for additional UTC key characteristics.)

INITIAL QUESTIONING

Recall the interview preparation plans you made after reading Chapter 2. Then start at the beginning of the applicant's career and work your way to the present—the opposite of the way most résumés and application forms are structured. This makes for a less choppy review of credentials, and permits an easier explication and measurement of professional progress.

At Pratt & Whitney, interviewers for executive hires use questions correlated with the six evaluation categories listed in Chapter 2. Each question probes specific qualities that have shaped an individual's background. Here are typical questions used by Pratt & Whitney interviewers for the Achievement category:

◆ Comment on your use of established objectives in accomplishing work results.

◆ Provide examples of your accomplishment of important objectives and explain how they contributed to the success of your unit and the company.

◆ What are the most formidable barriers you have encountered in accomplishing your work? What do you do about them?

◆ At what point do you conclude that a particular work objective has been completed?

◆ Provide an example of when your persistence paid off in achieving your goal, or when it didn't work out.

In a similar vein, Management Recruiters, an executive recruitment firm with offices nationwide, has prepared a guide to help its clients interpret the answers to interview questions in a number of areas. On page 50—slightly modified for our purposes—are samples of such interview questions, and the questions *behind* the questions. Perhaps there are ways you can apply this strategy to your own recruitment procedure.

(You Ask) MOTIVATION (You mean)

How will this job help you get what you want?	What are your priorities?
What have you done to prepare yourself for a better job?	How motivated are you?

INITIATIVE

How did you get into this line of work?	Are you a self-starter?
When have you felt like giving up on a task? Tell me about it.	Can you complete an unpleasant assignment?

INSIGHT

What is the most useful criticism you've received? From whom? Tell me about it. Most useless?	Can you take constructive action on your weaknesses?
How do you handle faultfinders?	How do you take criticism?

PLANNING

Give me an idea of how you spend a typical day.	Will you fit easily into our corporate culture and organizational structure?
If you were boss, how would you run your present job?	Do you have vision, or will you get bogged down by detail?

The senior recruiter of a New York electronics firm leans heavily on a book called *Hiring a Top Salesperson* to augment her situational interviewing style. "Whenever I go into an interview, I know what I want to get out of it. There are questions I need to ask—information I must get. But my first objective is to get a conversation going and relax the candidate.

"Next, I ask questions that highlight the personality or job-related trait I happen to be looking for. Let's take learning ability. I try to tie the questions to standards of performance. Centering on trait-related questions allows me to do that and still stay flexible in the interview.

"For example, here are some questions to identify a self-starter—a classic sales trait: 'What do you do to build a list of possible customers?' or, 'What did you do to prepare for this interview?'"

CLARIFYING ANSWERS

Probe until you are completely satisfied with an answer given by an applicant. Some questions that will help to clarify responses include the following:

◆ Why do you feel that way?

◆ Anything else?

◆ Why do you say that?

◆ What do you think causes that?

◆ Why did it turn out that way?

◆ Why was that such a disappointment to you?

◆ Can you give me another example?

Not responding to an answer will indicate that you expect a more thorough response. Resist the temptation to rephrase a question to make it easier for the applicant to reply. If you have prepared your questions thoroughly, the burden should fall on the applicant to provide full and satisfactory responses.

ENDING THE INTERVIEW

This is sometimes an awkward time for inexperienced interviewers, particularly if the occasion has been unpleasant for one or both parties. The most direct approach is simply to say something like: "Well, I've asked all of the questions I need to. Is there anything more you'd like to say or ask me?"

When all appropriate information has been exchanged, and you think you'd like to see the candidate again, address the following issues:

1. Be sure the candidate's interest in the position is high enough to justify further discussion.

2. Describe the decision making process for the position being filled. Tell the candidate approximately how many more people are scheduled to be interviewed, and over what time frame.

3. Let the candidate know approximately when to expect a call to schedule the next interview.

Applicants who do not make the first cut can be let down easily. Simply say that you will be talking with other people over the next few days (or weeks), and that everyone will be contacted at the conclusion of this process, whether they are invited back or not. Thank all candidates for their time and their interest in your company.

There is no specific number of interviews that guarantees an ideal selection process. In most cases, a large number of candidates are interviewed only once, and then are either hired or rejected. In many instances, though, more than one person is required to pass judgment on an applicant. Usually, the larger the department, the more interviewers there are in the process. This should be perceived as prudent, not bureaucratic. The people a prospective employee will interact with on a daily basis should have as much input in the selection process as possible.

You may want to screen applicants by conducting telephone interviews with applicants who live some distance away; this will save you money and save the applicant time. But this tactic is effective primarily for evaluating such traits as confidence, verbal skills, and job-related accomplishments. You will not have the luxury of seeing the person on the other end of the line, so factors such as body language, facial expression, eye contact, and neatness of appearance will have to be judged when you meet the applicants who survive this step of the hiring process.

Chapter 4

Evaluating the Interview:

Tools to Facilitate the Decision Making Process

"Whenever two people meet there are really six people present. There is each man as he sees himself, each man as the other person sees him, and each man as he really is."

—William James

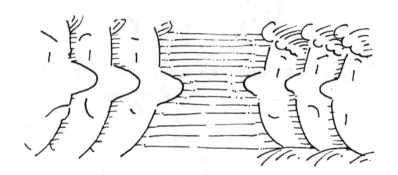

Evaluating an interview really begins with the application form and the résumé. But our focus is the interview itself, so let's begin there.

Knowing specifically the type of person you're looking for, based on the job description and other criteria, is job one. Next is being able to measure the quality of the candidate—both intrinsically and against all competitors. That is the subject of this chapter.

For a position requiring the review of dozens of applicants, reliance on memory alone is folly. So are random notes taken unsystematically during the interview. The rating system you use to sort out the strengths and weaknesses of applicants should reflect your organization's needs, culture, and policies.

One of your most important tasks as a recruiter is protecting against your own biases. Intellectually you know that your first impressions of a job applicant should have only proportional effect on your decision making. However, ensuring that this is so requires some effort on your part.

Remember "First impression and intuition, the twin gods of hiring decisions," described in Chapter 1? These are the principal villains when evaluative standards go haywire. Reliance on either one leads to a subjective rather than an objective judgment—antithetical to sound assessment of job candidates. For example, some interviewers may reject a bearded applicant before he says hello. At the other extreme, an outgoing, pleasant interviewee who has worked for the same employer as her interviewer may be able to take up enough time with anecdotal conversation to avoid substantive discussion of credentials. Here is the rule: Don't confuse *ability* with *likability.*

We've already seen how certain cultural, social, and physical considerations can stand in the way of the fair assessment of job applicants if they are unrelated to an ability to do the job. Keep in mind that rejecting an applicant—either consciously or unconsciously—for any reasons not directly related to job-performance ability may violate EEO regulations.

Objectivity on the part of the interviewer is essential for proper evaluation of a candidate in three areas:

◆ Experience—to assess ability to handle the open position

◆ Character—to anticipate reactions to job-related ethical and moral dilemmas

◆ Intellect—to predict problem solving ability and growth potential

RATING SYSTEMS

Recall for a moment Pratt & Whitney's executive selection model discussed in Chapter 2, and the questions relating to the "high performance standards" success characteristic (one of three such characteristics under the category labeled "Leading by Example"). Here is a way evaluators can interpret the range of answers they receive to those questions:

LOW

◆ There are serious problems with the performance standards set by this person—too severe, unrealistic, irrelevant, erratic (constantly changing, pedestrian, etc.).

◆ Exhibits little or no interest in setting performance standards; lets people set their own standards, and then settles for whatever they set.

◆ Sets double standards or unfair standards (e.g., doesn't hold self to the standards he or she expects from other people, sets or enforces standards subjectively, plays favorites, etc.).

◆ Does not set high or even average performance standards for himself or herself.

◆ Is not at all interested in competitive results, either in business or in personal pursuits.

AVERAGE

◆ Shows some interest in competition, but is not preoccupied with it.

◆ Is definitely achievement oriented, but the soundness of the standards he or she sets is at times questionable—may be unrealistically high or so low that they are easily achieved by everyone.

◆ Personal attention to achievement is not consistent—is achievement oriented part of the time, and is indifferent to achievement part of the time.

◆ Is satisfied with average or typical performance from others.

HIGH

◆ Is extremely competitive, as evidenced in business and personal pursuits.

◆ Sets quite demanding, yet achievable, performance expectations for himself or herself.

◆ Has quite demanding but fair performance expectations of others.

◆ Defines and gets agreement to performance standards that cause people to "stretch" to reach them.

◆ Consistently preoccupied with high achievement and with outstanding performance in all facets of his or her life—business, recreation, and personal.

◆ Sets performance standards at approximately 80 percent probability of success—high enough so that perfect success is not always achieved, but realistic enough so that they are reached most of the time.

(Answer evaluations to two other Success Characteristic question sets are listed on pages 100 and 102–103 of the Appendix.)

Less rigorous than the Pratt & Whitney model, but perhaps adequate for your needs, is a rating system devised by financial recruiter Robert Half. This system helps managers emphasize two intangible but important factors: innate ability and motivation. Five "Qualification" categories are weighted by value for a total of 10 (Experience, Education, Intelligence, Appearance, and Personality—and an additional category that varies with the position being filled). Each of these is multiplied by a value score ranging between

0 and 10 to achieve a rating for the five categories. (A sample form is included on page 101 of the Appendix.)

Tie Breakers

Candidates who score high in the various selection criteria may be better interviewees than they are candidates; that is, they may simply be adept at presenting themselves in a favorable light. Other factors that can help to identify the ideal candidate—particularly if verbal acuity is only part of the job description—include nonproprietary work samples and trial assignments.

Be prepared for this step to take some time. One manufacturing executive recalled the final stages in selecting a person for a tax department position some time ago. After three months of interviewing and evaluating candidates, he says, the search was reduced to two candidates, judged to be almost equal in qualifications. Several additional assignments were given to determine the best person. One of the two candidates finally said in exasperation: "Can't we just shoot baskets to decide this thing?" (He got the job—and not, said the executive, just because of his sense of humor.)

Selling the Organization

Presumably some time will have been spent early in the interview describing the organization and placing it in an industry context. If early interviews have gone well and a candidate is under serious consideration, it is time to talk in some detail about attributes that make your firm a desirable place to work. This is often a forgotten part of the interview. More than one offer has been rejected because a company recruiter took for granted the organization's positive aspects and neglected to cover them during the various interviews.

Companies with a strong sense of public image will be able to present themselves in part through their printed materials—annual reports, promotional literature, and product description brochures, for example. These, as well as verbal descriptions of whatever advantages your company is able to offer, can help you present your company as a desirable employer.

Be careful not to withhold any relevant negative aspects of the institution that candidates will learn on their own after they join it. This will only erode any trust that has been established, and perhaps sour the working relationship permanently.

Describing the company and its expectations in detail also makes possible the identification of candidates who may not fit in with the corporate culture—an intangible but important factor to consider. A career transition and corporate outplacement program called JOB-BRIDGE counsels recently terminated employees on ways to analyze corporate culture from *their* perspective, through probing questioning of the interviewer. JOB-BRIDGE's authors describe corporate culture this way:

> *A corporate culture is a powerful force, impervious to individual pressure—or even group pressure—to change. Corporate norms affect an individual's attitude and performance from a number of different perspectives. They occur in such areas as information sharing (it either is a norm or it isn't), innovation (it's either encouraged or it isn't), self-expression, and socialization with one's work group.*

> *Industrial psychologists have identified two basic types of corporate culture. In a "closed" corporate culture, as described in a study by Professor Ralph*

H. Kilmann of the University of Pittsburgh, work units guard their fiefdoms carefully and share little information. They protect themselves at all times, minimizing risk-taking and generally exhibiting extreme caution. An "adaptive" corporation, on the other hand, requires both risk and trust. Employees actively support one another's efforts to identify problems and reach solutions.

Individuals who don't tune in quickly to the many nuances of their corporation's culture usually find themselves in deep trouble. Those who are patient and clever enough to go through the motions can survive until they are able to find a position with another company in which the culture is more in tune with their own work habits, attitudes, and style. Mavericks who think they can buck or change the system, however, are in for a rough time. Without compromise, in fact, their paydays definitely are numbered.[1]

---

[1]*Job-Bridge.* © Wilson McLeran, Inc. New Haven, CT 06511

Look for ways to introduce this topic in the selection interview after you are sure you can define your own corporate culture. Go into as much detail as necessary about behavior and attitudes your company values—as well as the extent to which a new employee would have to change his or her existing behavior and attitudes—to determine whether the fit is a good one. Hiring a well-qualified individual who may also be a latent "corporate misfit" is not only expensive, but ultimately painful to both employee and employer.

Finally, find out about the feelings of the prospective employee's family, particularly if the position requires that the family relocate. The prospective employee may neglect to thoroughly discuss the new position with his or her spouse. Uncommunicated objections and resentments on the part of the "trailing spouse" that surface only at decision time kill thousands of hires every year.

REFERENCE CHECKING

One of the most delicate stages in the hiring process is that of contacting a candidate's former employers for assessments of background and character. Until recently, the difficulty lay largely with determining the objectivity of the reference. A person who left his or her last job under difficult circumstances and whose boss was vindictive might suffer disproportionately. A former employer who was also a friend could deny the existence of any job-related problems. The impact of skewed references such as these was often reduced by simply getting more of them.

Those were the uncomplicated days. Then came a raft of invasion-of-privacy lawsuits against employers trying to get information about applicants. These still occur, of course, but another ingredient has been added. Now, courts may even hold employers liable for "negligent hiring," or under-investigating. Albert

Zakarian, a lawyer at Day, Berry & Howard, in Hartford, Connecticut, calls negligent hiring suits "among the most important legal developments for employers in the last ten years."

An extreme, real-life example: An apartment-complex owner in Minnesota hired a manager without checking references. One day the new manager entered a resident's apartment and raped her. The woman sued the employer and won. The court felt that the owner, had he checked, would have learned that the manager had a criminal record for violent assault. The fact that the manager lied on his application form was deemed irrelevant, because the information could have been checked and was not.

A hypothetical variation of this situation illustrates a different problem. Let's say the apartment-complex owner checked with his manager-applicant's former employers, who did not divulge information about the man's criminal record. The owner could then in turn sue the former employer for withholding such information. (The catch-22 here is that employing an ex-convict is not considered to be negligent hiring *per se,* because there is reason to believe that once released from jail a person has been rehabilitated—either totally or partially.)

Several rules of thumb apply in getting information about a prospective employee that avoids potential legal entanglements. Remember, however, that not all will apply to your particular situation.

◆ Require a signed statement certifying the truth of all application and résumé entries, with termination as the penalty for falsification.

◆ Ask probing questions during interviews to shed light on past problems: "Have you ever been fired—why? Have you ever been passed up for promotion—why?"

- ◆ Require a waiver from the prospective employee for permission from former employers to release specifically identified information.

- ◆ Restrict all queries about a candidate to job-related requirements.

- ◆ For the most accurate and candid information about a prospective employee, choose as references the immediate supervisors of the candidate, or the person above the immediate supervisor.

- ◆ Consider hiring professional reference checkers—especially to uncover such public documents as police records, driving records, and real estate records, which can be time-consuming.

- ◆ Remember the concept of "qualified privilege," which in most states offers references a safe harbor for truthful information given in good faith.

◆ Confidentiality is essential. Discuss reference-check information only with other employees actively involved in the hiring process.

Executive recruiter Robert Half recommends nine "tough questions" for references, to help you through the final stage of candidate assessment:

1. How would you compare the candidate's performance to that of the person doing the job now? Or: What characteristics will you look for in a replacement?

2. If she was that good, why didn't you try to induce her to stay?

3. When there was a particularly urgent assignment, what steps did he take to get it done on time?

4. Since none of us is perfect, please describe some areas in which he could improve.

5. Have you seen her current résumé? Let me read you the part that describes her job with your organization. (Stop at each significant point, and ask the reference for a comment.)

6. Not all employees get along well together. What kinds of people did he or she have trouble with?

7. On the average, how many times a month does she take off for personal reasons or sickness? How many times a month does she come in late or leave early?

8. Who referred him to your organization?

9. When she was hired, were her references checked thoroughly? Who checked these references? What did the references have to say?

Chapter 5

Job Offer and Compensation Negotiation:

Final Steps Leading to Hire

*"To love what you do and feel that it matters—
how could anything be more fun?"*

—Katharine Graham

As we have seen in the preceding chapters, considerable time and effort are necessary to define and structure a position, and then find and attract the right person to fill it. Preparing and presenting the job offer are crucial parts of any hire. Yet, ironically, less attention is given to the job offer, proportionately, than to any other aspect of the process. This is significant when one realizes that failure at this stage *without qualified backup candidates* means repeating the entire process from the beginning.

One of the most common reasons for failure at this critical point is *psychological.* The employer assumes that the hard part of the process is over, and that the only step remaining is the candidate's acceptance. The candidate, however, is relishing star treatment perhaps rarely experienced, fantasizing a compensation package more generous than the one offered.

Not that the employer is always blameless at this stage. Let's look at an oft-played scenario. Assume that structured compensation ranges exist for all exempt and nonexempt positions at a company. Depending on the candidate's qualifications and current compensation, the hiring authority should be able to develop a formula for a mutually acceptable offer. But when the employer misreads—or, worse, fails to fulfill—the candidate's expectations, the deal can fall apart. One of the biggest reasons for employing executive recruiters is that they serve as interpreters for both sides' positions.

A candidate interested in a job change even before beginning deliberations with your company probably has talked with other companies as well. This could mean a bidding war with one or more of your competitors. The new hire you are thinking of as almost "on the payroll" could be using your offer as a bludgeon to force more money out of his or her current employer. These and other hidden agendas must be dealt with during the offer stage to minimize the undoing of all of your hard work and planning.

STRUCTURING THE OFFER

In his book *Successful Negotiation,* Robert Maddux, a management consultant with THinc. Consulting Group International, recommends six basic steps that he believes ensure mutual agreement between a job applicant and the company making the offer. These steps are broadly applicable to most hiring situations:

1. Get to know the party with whom you will be negotiating.

2. Share your goals and objectives with the other party.

3. Study all of the issues before negotiations begin, to determine where any advantages or drawbacks may lie.

4. After the issues have been defined, express any areas of disagreement or conflict.

5. Reassess your position to see what level of compromise is acceptable.

6. Affirm any agreements that have been reached. Put the agreement in writing, when applicable, and share it with the other side.

Successful compensation negotiation is achieved when *win/win attitudes* prevail on both sides. Both parties have to be willing to give up something to get what they want, or *most* of what they want. Compromise is in everybody's best interest. The employer wants the individual badly enough to make an offer in the first place and the candidate is interested enough to hear what the prospective employer has to say.

Structuring the offer requires a sensitivity to the needs of the new employee—economic, motivational, and psychological—within the constraints of company precepts. All nonnegotiable issues involving company policy should be dealt with immediately, to avoid both time-wasting haggling and misunderstanding. Some benefits and relocation issues, for example, may be at odds with the candidates' expectations, but may also be the product of strict company policy, with no basis for compromise. A human resource representative is best qualified to describe the complete company benefits package and respond to all questions.

SALARY AND BONUS

Next comes base salary. Most positions have a built-in range that accommodates the hire of individuals with differing experience levels and salary requirements. A starting salary should allow for and reflect the potential for employee growth in that position for at least three years.

Base salaries tend to reflect the cost of living in various parts of the country as well. This may have to be pointed out to a candidate who is relocating—from Chicago to Austin, Texas, for example. In the late 1990s, a dollar is going more than 15 percent further in Austin than in Chicago, and the differential in real estate costs between the two cities is even greater. All such variables should be realistically ascertained and introduced into the salary negotiations when appropriate.

Often there is only marginal room for negotiating a base salary because of company policy constraints; if so, these constraints should be set forth as early as possible.

Incentive bonuses based on the employee's performance (as reflected in departmental or division revenue or profit performance) obviously are a valuable bargaining chip, but company policy may restrict any tampering with existing formulas and limit your negotiating latitude in this area. Be sure to fully describe any incentive bonus plans, including pay increases that reflect promotion to higher levels.

One incentive being used more and more frequently is the *sign-on bonus*. Sign-on bonuses are useful in raising the total compensation figure without affecting the base salary structure, helping a candidate who otherwise would come in well over the midpoint of your salary range to meet his or her first-year goals.

For some executive hires, it may be prudent to formalize final negotiations with a contract or letter of agreement. Such a document may include any or all of the following provisions:

1. term or duration of employment

2. description of duties

3. base salary

4. performance bonuses of various kinds

5. medical, dental, and life insurance

6. retirement benefits

7. relocation expenses where applicable (sometimes to include company purchase and disposition of the old residence, and/or company assumption of closing costs of the new residence)

8. low- or no-interest loans

9. periodic payment of company-related expenses of various kinds

10. "luxury perks," such as limousines and country club memberships

11. contingency clauses (often called "golden parachutes") in the event of a change in company ownership

12. severance conditions (amount, frequency, and duration)

13. contract termination conditions (for both employer and employee)

The Counteroffer

Behind every offer is the possibility of a counteroffer from the company the candidate is leaving. Some candidates may be courting such offers, but with little intention of leaving their current employers. Some people who have been with their firm for a number of years feel the need to test their marketability with a competitor, or see what compensation they can command on the open market.

In many cases an employer is shocked to learn that a key manager has been offered employment elsewhere and uses whatever weapons are at hand—money being foremost among them—to overturn the decision. Executive recruiters are well aware of this danger, and usually make sure they cover counteroffers in preliminary discussions with candidates under serious consideration. Many employers who recruit on their own are unlikely to worry about counteroffers until they have been burned one time and realize the amount of work that must be redone to hire a person as qualified as the person they have failed to land.

Most counteroffers are tainted because of the circumstances under which they are proffered. A company in a crisis situation of one kind or another may indeed need the departing manager—but only until the crisis abates. After that time, the manager becomes damaged goods and vulnerable to being terminated.

Written Follow Up

Every offer, except those for entry- or low-level positions, should be confirmed in writing. Be sure to include the start date, title, salary, relocation terms (if applicable), and any other specific conditions mutually agreed to.

Conversely, unsuccessful candidates, especially those in a protracted or rigorous selection process, should be given the courtesy of a written response. Good candidates who don't quite fit the available opening may be ideal for an opening that surfaces a few months from now. (A selection of sample offers and rejection letters can be found on pages 104–107 of the Appendix.)

Chapter 6

♦

Other Job-Related Interviews:

*Performance Evaluation, Voluntary
and Involuntary Termination Meetings*

"A man is a success if he gets up in the morning and gets to bed at night, and in between he does what he wants to."

—Bob Dylan

In addition to selection interviews, you will be asked from time to time to conduct three other types of interviews. One measures the progress of individuals in your company; another takes place when an employee leaves your company. The third type of interview is rarely planned, but is an excellent opportunity for gathering intelligence about your industry and competing companies. The three types of interviews are:

◆ the performance evaluation interview

◆ the exit interview

◆ the information interview

THE PERFORMANCE EVALUATION INTERVIEW

Job performance appraisal usually is conducted on an annual basis. Some companies conduct performance reviews semiannually. Many experts agree that evaluation offered informally on a continuing basis as an ongoing communication tool is the most effective type. Proper use of this lightning rod can go a good distance toward balancing the company's need to develop productive employees with the employee's need for constructive, objective feedback.

The interview portion of any performance appraisal should consist of a thorough review of the employee's goals for the period, examine the degree to which they were accomplished, and establish goals for the subsequent period. Of course, this presupposes that clear goals exist and have been agreed to by the employee.

Such a critical event—for both employee and employer—requires both thorough preparation and a careful *prioritization of objectives*. It is important to suppress whatever discomfort you have over judging others so that your feelings don't adversely affect the outcome of the meeting. (Keep the interview in perspective: you are judging *performance*, after all, not the entire person.)

Preparing for the evaluation interview:

◆ Review all relevant documents to familiarize yourself with the employee's total performance. Keep a folder on each employee in which you can file work samples and notes related to the employee's record.

◆ Schedule all performance reviews at least one week in advance to allow employees—as well as yourself—time to become fully prepared.

◆ Prepare an agenda for the meeting, and share it in advance with the employee. Possible sequence:

1. statement of objectives;

2. employee self-assessment (achievements, problems, professional growth paths);

3. manager response;

4. causes of any problems explored by both;

5. objectives and plan for next review period set by both.

◆ Keep the review system simple. It should be easy for managers to use and easy for employees to understand.

◆ Use evaluation interviews to give positive as well as negative feedback for more effective career growth.

Conducting the appraisal interview:

◆ Hold the meeting where you and the employee can sit face-to-face—without a desk between you, or on the same side of the desk. Attempt to minimize your "authority figure" role; this will improve the free flow of information. Set a tone for an open discussion.

◆ Select for discussion only those accomplishments and problems that will make a real difference in the evaluation. A long list of trivial behavior problems will probably not be absorbed, and will discourage improved performance.

◆ Focus feedback on behavior rather than on the person.

◆ Focus on the amount and kind of information an employee can use, rather than on the amount of information you want to give.

◆ Focus feedback on behavior relating to specific situations, rather than on abstract characteristics.

◆ Get employee commitment to performance improvement goals. Get the employee to state how the goals will be accomplished.

◆ Be succinct, objective, and clear in all writing connected with performance reviews.

Avoiding appraisal interview pitfalls:

◆ Ask others who have observed the employee to share their observations with you.

◆ Create a nonthreatening self-assessment climate; assure employees that the interview will be closer to a discussion than a court proceeding.

◆ Be sure you are aware of any recent changes in personnel, scheduling, or project composition that could make the job easier or more difficult than you originally thought.

◆ Be aware of personal biases that may affect your evaluation. Try to dismiss any generalizations you may have developed regarding individuals or groups, so as not to over- or underrate.

◆ Try to allow for individual differences in your ratings of employees interviewed in tandem. Don't judge a competent (but average) employee by the same standards as a superstar in the evaluation session just concluded.

◆ Rate honestly, rather than "right down the middle" to avoid appearing either tough or soft. Boosting low ratings hides problems; reducing high ratings kills self-confidence and motivation.

◆ Utilize reviews on a continuing basis as guidelines for coaching. Give regular feedback on progress to assist in goals reassessment.

EXIT INTERVIEWS

The days of lifetime employment in a single company are, with very few exceptions, over. What this means is that sooner or later just about everyone moves on—some of their own volition, others under duress of various kinds. Either way, it is important that no one leave your company without being interviewed by his or her manager, or a representative of the human resources department. Those who have resigned must be replaced, a process that costs the company not only dollars and time, but often morale as well.

Those who have been severed from your organization, however, must be told so. This is done either just before or as part of the termination interview.

Voluntary Departures

Anybody who leaves the employ of your company can tell you something that may make less likely the loss of other people. Unfortunately, you are not likely to hear about any problems if you are the manager to whom your recent defector reported. You may have been the cause of the departure—but a person who reported to you is not likely to admit it on the way out the door. This is natural. After all, few people want to burn bridges or indict a boss.

Most employees who depart voluntarily are reluctant to say anything negative in the exit interview, and are likely to give as the reason for their departure "a better opportunity." It is your job to get through this veneer and unearth possible personnel or organizational problems that may be contributing to high turnover.

The creative director at a West Coast division of a large advertising agency had made life miserable for his second in command for almost a year. One Monday morning she found her office taken over by the art director, with her furniture crammed into his former—and smaller—office.

Although she enjoyed her work and did it well, she reluctantly concluded that it was time to leave, and accepted a lateral position with a Boston agency. Several years later she ran into the president of her former division at a trade show. He said he would have promoted her to creative director had she stayed, having long since fired the nemesis boss. She then mentioned the circumstances under which she left, and both were surprised at the way the world worked. Would a thorough exit interview have changed things? Maybe not, but it would have shed light on an extremely unhealthy work situation, and perhaps saved the jobs of others victimized by the tyrant boss.

One way to avoid situations like this is to volunteer to conduct exit interviews as a courtesy for departing employees who report to *other* managers, and ask that these managers do the same for you. Another solution is to turn the whole job over to your human resources department.

Here are some ways to get the most out of the assignment and help to reduce turnover in your company. You'll have to be at your best to get value from exit interviews. The mind-set of most people in this situation is that they are there only to be coerced out of their decision, which results in varying degrees of defensiveness. Vicki LaFarge, a management professor at Bentley College in Boston, Massachusetts, recommends beginning the session with a few softballs: "I see you've been here six years. What kind of assignments have you had?" Then, says LaFarge, once a rapport has developed, zero in more closely on the job itself and its pluses and minuses. For example:

◆ "What did you like most about working here?" "What did you like least?"

◆ "If you were a consultant to this company, what would you recommend?"

◆ "What was it like working for Randy Williams?" If the answer is vague or euphemistic: "On the grounds that nobody is perfect, what would have made Randy a better boss, in your opinion?"

◆ "Where are you going to be working?" "How does the job sound?" (a good way to obtain intelligence about your competitors). "How did you hear about the position?" (a way to learn which executive recruiters or employment agencies are raiding your company).

To get the most out of an exit interview, probe for specific details after each answer—without passing judgment on the response. At the end of a nonproductive meeting, leave the door open for follow-up conversations. The emotional and psychic distance that three to six months away from the company can give the departing employee may make follow-up discussions much more productive.

The Termination Interview

Every manager dreads having to fire an employee, whatever the circumstances that have brought about the firing. The emotional trauma associated with termination, in fact, sometimes causes managers to delay the act much longer than is appropriate, with negative consequences that include missed deadlines, lost sales, and reduced morale. Mishandled terminations can also have legal, public relations, and business consequences.

The decision to terminate an employee should be made only when everything has been done to preclude it. People identified as marginal performers in previous evaluations should have been targeted for special attention—transfer, counseling, or other opportunities to correct the problem.

Terminations fall into three categories, with important distinctions among the three:

1. "For cause"—stealing, misrepresentation, unethical or dangerous behavior

2. Poor performance—failure to meet objectives, master required skills, or perform assigned tasks

3. Job elimination—merger or acquisition, regional or local economic conditions, business failure

Rarely are specific terminations as clear-cut as these categories suggest. Such intangibles as poor chemistry and favoritism are very often factors, but are sometimes euphemisms for more insidious reasons. Vindictive managers do exist, of course. Some are jealous, insecure, or fearful of competition from ambitious subordinates. Those managers whose performance itself is suspect may escape responsibility for the time being by firing a less powerful employee—in effect, making a scapegoat of the person terminated.

No matter which of the three categories applies, you should coordinate all terminations with the human resources department. Of course, policies vary from company to company—as do federal, state, and local regulations. Your human resources people can inform you as to appropriate pre- and post-termination actions, as well as regarding the firing itself.

Decisions to terminate an employee because of substandard performance should be carefully documented with individual performance appraisals and at least one written warning. Such documentation should go back at least six months; this will demonstrate that the employee has been advised of performance deficiencies and been given sufficient opportunity to correct them.

The following checklists will help you to prepare for and conduct termination interviews that respect employees' dignity, reduce managers' anxiety, and minimize company liability in the event of a legal proceeding arising from the termination:

PREPARING FOR THE INTERVIEW

◆ Notify and receive necessary approvals from the human resources department.

◆ Identify any potential employee physical problems for possible adverse reaction; have emergency resources on hand.

◆ Schedule an appointment with the employee (early in the day and early in the week are preferable).

◆ Arrange for the transition of all responsibilities and work in progress; schedule premises departure time and date.

◆ Arrange for the return of all company identification, keys, and confidential or proprietary materials.

◆ Assemble necessary documentation if the termination is performance related. If the termination is the result of a planned reduction in force, explain the rationale.

◆ Prepare all written severance information: notification letter, salary continuation/severance period, benefits, and outplacement counseling (if applicable).

◆ Prepare a brief message for the meeting, listing two or three reasons for the termination. Decide what you will tell remaining employees. (The entire meeting should last no longer than ten to fifteen minutes.)

◆ Prepare yourself emotionally for the meeting: discuss your feelings with human resources professionals; acknowledge your anxiety; don't assume personal responsibility for the termination decision.

◆ Anticipate the range of employee reactions (shock, anger, denial) and try to avoid defensive behavior. (See the Bibliography for books on ways to deal with possible employee reactions.)

CONDUCTING THE INTERVIEW

◆ The employee's immediate supervisor should conduct the meeting alone, or with a human resources representative present if company policy so dictates.

◆ Invite the employee to sit down. Avoid small talk and get right to the point.

◆ Deliver your message and listen to the employee's response.

◆ Explain that the decision is final, with no room for debate. Also explain that there is no other open position for the employee.

◆ Give the employee the notification letter or memorandum.

◆ Review all terms of the termination (unless they are being handled by human resources): notice period, salary continuation period; severance amount and period; benefit status; outplacement (if applicable).

◆ Discuss logistics of employee's departure: work flow; departure from work area; return of company identification, keys, and confidential or proprietary materials.

◆ Ask the employee if there are any questions. Restate terms, if necessary. Don't argue or become defensive.

◆ Close the meeting, and escort the employee to the next meeting, if applicable.

Information Interviews

Many job seekers are counseled to include information interviewing as part of a well-rounded job transition marketing plan. The strategy is to make contact with—and a positive impression on—a decision maker well connected enough to know where at least one good job is. You can expect that former colleagues or associates will give your name to any number of individuals looking for work. Often you can help a petitioner accomplish such a mission; more often, you cannot. There are several ways to extract a *quid pro quo* from courtesy meetings.

But every once in a while you'll get a request for a meeting from someone who has as much information to give as to receive. Ask to receive a résumé in advance of the meeting. Internalize any useful data relative to the individual's goals and also determine from the person's background what relevant information might parallel your own interests and priorities.

If you give freely of your time, experience, and contacts—and ask the right questions—you are likely to get as much as you give from the courtesy interview.

BIBLIOGRAPHY

Arthur, Diane, *Recruiting, Interviewing, Selecting, and Orienting New Employees,* second edition (New York, NY: AMACOM, 1991). Helpful information at every stage of the hire.

Drucher, Peter F., *Managing the Non-Profit Organization* (New York, NY: HarperCollins Publishers, 1990). "Offers managers in the non-profit sector the kind of vigorous, sensible, mind-stretching advice that has won him a reputation as the most stimulating management thinker of our time." *New York Times Book Review.*

Executive Compensation Reports (Alexandria, VA: DP Publications Co., twice-monthly newsletter). Reviews the compensation programs at more than 1,500 companies with annual revenues of $75 million or more. Articles disclose stock plans, compensation packages, and severance arrangements of named executives.

Fournies, Ferdinand F., *Coaching for Improved Work Performance* (Blue Ridge Summit, PA: Liberty House, 1987). Practical techniques for improving productivity, improving quality, gaining commitment, increasing employee involvement, and modifying behavior of subordinates.

Friedman, Martin, *Hiring a Top Salesperson* (Performance Design, 1989). Categorizes interview questions to more readily classify applicants by personality traits such as "self-starter" and "learning ability."

——, *333 Interviewing Questions* (Walnut Creek, CA: Borgman Associates, 1990). They're all here. Use the ones that fit your situation.

Interview Guide for Supervisors, fourth edition (Washington, DC: College and University Personnel Association, 1993). Sound information designed to assure effective hiring decisions. Includes legal considerations as well as all aspects of the employment selection process.

Morin, William, *Successful Termination* (New York, NY: Drake Beam Morin, Inc., 1989). Description of the range of possible employee reactions to termination, and effective strategies for dealing with each.

Tarrant, John, *Perks and Parachutes* (New York, NY: Simon & Schuster, 1985.) Teaches bargaining table psychology and strategy; how to negotiate the best employment package; examples of actual Fortune 500 company contracts.

Weiss, W. H., *Decision Making for First-Time Managers* (New York, NY: AMACOM, 1986). The essentials of decision making, factors that influence decisions, and solutions to a number of problem situations requiring decisive action.

Appendix

Interview Guides, Sample Evaluation Sheets,
Acceptance/Rejection Letters,
Permissible/Prohibited Inquiries,
Position Outline, and Job Application Forms

Donnelley Directory

▐▌ a company of
▐▌ the Dun & Bradstreet Corporation

THE SALES MANAGER'S INTERVIEW
GUIDE FOR SALES CANDIDATES

APPLICANT NAME	DATE

POSITION APPLIED FOR

INTERVIEWER'S NAME

The Interview Guide for Sales Candidates is designed to be flexible and easy to use. This guide is to be used by the sales manager. With this in mind, the format consists of the following:

SUGGESTED QUESTIONS: These questions parallel specific criteria determined to be necessary for success in a Donnelley Directory sales position. Feel free to use your own appropriate questions. It is not necessary to cover everything suggested here verbatim.

NOTES: Unstructured space for notes is provided to allow for note taking that follows the flow of your interview.

CHECKLIST & SUMMARY: The checklist and summary are provided to help you evaluate the results of your interview. It is suggested this be done immediately following the interview.

In addition to the information contained on the following pages, you should keep in mind the following important considerations:

- Avoid questions that elicit potentially discriminatory information (race, religion, national origin, age, sex, handicap, marital status).

- While it may be appropriate to question educational experience, requirement of a degree for a Sales Candidate is not appropriate.

- Use of open-ended questions (who, what, when, where, how).

- Be attentive to non-verbals, i.e., eye contact, gestures, the way the candidate sits, etc.

- Be attentive to voice quality, i.e., tone, inflection, emphasis, pauses, rate of speech, etc.

- Can we verify the information by reference checks or by other means?

- Did the applicant come prepared with questions and/or knowledge about Donnelley Directory?

REMEMBER: Completion of this guide is one aspect of the interviewing process. Review the applicant's résumé, application, and the Personnel Completed Patterned Interview Form prior to your interview. *All* forms on *all* candidates should be returned to Personnel once the hiring decision has been made.

I. WORK EXPERIENCE

FACTORS TO CONSIDER

—Is the information you've obtained based on the objective observations that can be verified?
—Is the information consistent with the résumé and/or the application?
—Did each new job logically build and expand upon the previous work assignment leading to increased responsibility? Is there a pattern of success?
—Did the applicant have positive productive relationships with previous supervisors, clients, peers, and subordinates?
—How did the applicant follow the flow of the interview?

SUGGESTED QUESTIONS

1. Tell me about your previous work/sales experience.
2. With each job, what did you like most? Least?
3. What has contributed most to your career so far?
4. What setbacks or disappointments have you had in your career so far?

II. ADMINISTRATIVE ABILITY

FACTORS TO CONSIDER

—Did it appear that the candidate had done some background work on Donnelley Directory?
—Was the candidate prepared with questions? Was the candidate on time?
—How has the applicant planned or organized the coverage of his present market?
—Tolerance for paperwork.
—How well were the candidate's thoughts organized?

SUGGESTED QUESTIONS

1. ORGANIZING/TIME MANAGEMENT

—How do you organize your sales day in your current job or your last job?
—How do you set up your week or day?
—How many prospects are available now (i.e. How many in your total assignment?) How many can you cover weekly, monthly, annually?
—If you were given a sales assignment with X number accounts, what would you do?

2. PLANNING

—How do you/would you plan for a sales call?
—What do you know about Donnelley Directory?

III. SALES QUALITIES

SUGGESTED QUESTIONS

1. COMPETITIVENESS/NEED FOR RECOGNITION
—What was your ranking/performance in your previous position(s)?
—How did you compare to others?
—Do you have sales bulletins or letters of commendation?
—What was your class ranking?
—Tell me about your outside activities.

2. CREATIVITY
—Tell how you have or would creatively make a difficult sale.

3. ENERGY LEVEL
—Describe a normal work day.
—How many calls do you/have you made in a day? What is the average length of your calls?
—How many sales do you currently close in a day?
—How do you spend your free time?

4. GOAL-ORIENTATION/DESIRE TO EXCEL
—Tell me about your goals.
—Tell me about your accomplishments/awards. Any documentation?
—What goals have you set for yourself and met?
—Did applicant talk about taking charge? About being No. 1?
—How do you measure your success and your growth?

5. INITIATIVE/SELF-STARTER
—What are your outside interests?
—How did you get this interview?

6. SELF-DISCIPLINE/INDEPENDENCE
—Explain how you work with others.
—Describe how you work independently.
—Have you been attending school while working? Explain.
—Have you ever owned your own business? Explain.
—How does applicant deal with rejection?

7. EARNINGS NEED/MONEY MOTIVATION
—What have your earnings been?
—How have earnings been made up? (base/commission/bonus)
—Is applicant money motivated?

8. COMMUNICATION/PERSUASIVENESS
—What were non-verbals like? Did the candidate lean forward?
—Did applicant ask questions, ask for feedback, elaborate on answers?
—Is applicant persuasive?
—Is he/she hard to hear?
—Is candidate assertive?
—Are general communication skills effective?

IV. OTHER FACTORS

SUGGESTED QUESTIONS

1. FLEXIBILITY/POSITIVE ATTITUDE
—Tell me about your former employers.
—How do you handle difficult co-workers or managers?
—How would you react to last minute changes in your assignment?

2. WILLINGNESS TO ACCEPT RESPONSIBILITY
—How much responsibility do you have now? Is it enough?
—How much responsibility can you handle?

3. EDUCATION (IF APPLICABLE)
—Why did you choose the major you chose? Has it helped your career?

4. ACCURACY
—How are errors measured in your current position?
—Where do you stand?
—Which is more important—quality or quantity?

5. MANAGEMENT POTENTIAL/DESIRE
—Have you ever managed people?
—What are management characteristics of a previous manager that you thought were effective? Ineffective?
—Tell me about your best/worst boss.

CHECKLIST AND SUMMARY

APPLICANT'S NAME _____ DATE _____

PLEASE EVALUATE THE FOLLOWING CRITERIA FOR THIS APPLICANT

	NOT ACCEPTABLE	LESS THAN ACCEPTABLE	ACCEPTABLE	MORE THAN ACCEPTABLE
I. WORK EXPERIENCE (Including earnings, comparable experience, level of responsibility, management potential/desire if applicable, etc.)	☐	☐	☐	☐
II. ADMINISTRATIVE ABILITY (Including time management, planning, organizing)	☐	☐	☐	☐

III. SALES QUALITIES

1. Competitiveness □ □ □ □
2. Creativity □ □ □ □
3. Energy Level □ □ □ □
4. Goal Orientation □ □ □ □
5. Initiative □ □ □ □
6. Self-Discipline/Independence □ □ □ □
7. Earnings need/Money motivated □ □ □ □
8. Communication/Persuasiveness □ □ □ □

IV. OTHER FACTORS
(Explain) □ □ □ □

RECOMMEND

□ HIRE

□ NO HIRE

□ FURTHER
INFORMATION
REQUIRED

COMMENTS

Leadership Associates Program
Candidate Evaluation Sheet

CANDIDATE _____

INTERVIEWER _____

DATE _____

RATING CODE

5-Outstanding
3-Average
1-Low

CHARACTERISTIC :	COMMENTS	: RANKING
LEADERSHIP Achievement Risk Taker	Reference her experience with a team project – she saw it as demanding and not without pitfalls. I was impressed with her candor and perception. She accurately believes she must earn leadership.	4
INTERPERSONAL Team Leadership Respect for People	She delves into problems with the goal of making the solutions winners for everyone. She cited her Digital Assignment as integrating design and manufacturing through personal involvement.	5
PERSONAL Principled Courage of Convictions	Strong beliefs that incorporate an understanding of diverse cultural foundations. Demonstrated a toughness to hang in and achieve through results. Sees modesty as strength.	4
COMMUNICATIONS Oral Communications Listening Skills	Articulate, enthusiastic. Handled complex questions well. Took full advantage of the hour to sell herself as well as get her questions answered.	4
INTELLECTUAL Reasoning Intelligent	Intelligent, analytical, and curious – all of which can only improve with practical experience.	4

RECOMMENDED ACTION
EXTEND OFFER FOR L.A.P. ✓ YES ___ NO
Note: Mentioned offer from Kodak and interview with GE.

21

TOTAL

ROBERT HALF®

Half's Interviewing Record and Evaluation
H-I-R-E

CANDIDATE'S NAME		POSITION		DATE	TIME	
SALARY	ASKS	EARNS	WILL PROBABLY ACCEPT			
QUALIFICATIONS	(1) VALUES Assign values to each qualification. Total must equal 10.	(2) RATINGS-Your rating of candidate on basis of 0 to 10 for each qualification.		(3) EVALUATION Multiply all values in Col. (1) by ratings in Col. (2).	COMMENTS	
EXPERIENCE		×	=			
EDUCATION		×	=			
INTELLIGENCE		×	=			
APPEARANCE & PERSONALITY		×	=			
OTHER		×	=			
TOTAL	10	TOTAL EVALUATION (Maximum 100)	(4)	(5)		
ADJUSTED EVALUATION INDEX. Rate candidate's *innate ability* and *motivation* on the basis of 1 to 10.						
ADJUSTED EVALUATION. Multiply (5) x (4) maximum 1,000.			(6)			

This copyright system is the most effective method of comparing candidates for a position. The interviewer predetermines the relative importance of each qualification, and then rates each candidate accordingly. This results in an evaluation of how closely a candidate conforms to the qualifications. The interviewer then adjusts the evaluation based on his or her impression of the candidate's *innate ability* and *motivation*.

BEHAVIORAL DESCRIPTIONS FOR UTC EXECUTIVE SUCCESS CHARACTERISTICS

Judge of People

LOW	AVERAGE	HIGH
• Has really been "fooled" a number of times by people—has greatly misjudged their qualifications or potential for success in a given assignment.	• Has a good "batting average" when it comes to judging people and making selection or assignment decisions— has enjoyed many successes but also a fair number of disappointments.	• Extremely insightful in discerning the strengths and deficiencies of people.
• Because of over-optimism or over-pessimism, this person does not accurately assess peoples' qualifications.	• Seems to do no better or no worse than most managers with respect to assessing people.	• Makes highly effective judgments concerning the employment and utilization of people—in many instances they surpass their own performance expectations.
• Appears to have a lower "batting average" than most managers when it comes to judging people.	• Has some "blind spots" when it comes to making judgments about people—there are some areas where he or she is not particularly perceptive.	• Has established an outstanding "track record" in identifying "winners."
• Puts people in assignments which do not make best use of their talents, resulting in frustration for them and in less than desired productivity for the organization.	• At times, may be overly optimistic or overly pessimistic about how someone will perform in a job or in a new assignment.	• Serves as an advisor to others in the organization concerning the assessment or deployment of people.
		• Has a real "knack" for placing people in situations where their talents will connect and permit them to "hit home runs."

1	2	3	4	5	6	7	8	9
DEFICIENCY			←		→		STRENGTH	

BEHAVIORAL DESCRIPTIONS FOR UTC EXECUTIVE SUCCESS CHARACTERISTICS

Business Vision

LOW

- Evidences a short-range, here-and-now, short-term point of view vis-à-vis the business.

- Gives lip-service to business vision, but presents no real evidence of the capability to articulate a business vision which others can understand and identify with.

- Evidences a narrow operational, functional, technical, or specialist point of view; has great difficulty conceiving or defining the business situation in general manager terms.

- Overlooks or does not understand how to define the profit potential in a future business state.

- Demonstrates an incomplete or erroneous understanding of the dynamics of the business.

- Has major "blind spots" with respect to market opportunities or key factors in the competititve situation.

AVERAGE

- Able to express a direction for the business that extends beyond a year.

- Recognizes business opportunities and major aspects of the competitive situation.

- May or may not adequately address the profit issue as an integral part of the business direction.

- Capably outlines the major components of future business state.

- Most efforts undertaken are related to the business outcome he or she is trying to achieve.

- Has an understanding of the dynamics of the business, but has difficulty expressing an explicit definition of where the business should go.

HIGH

- Clearly articulates a longer-term direction for the business.

- Takes into account key market opportunities, the significant components of the competitive situation, and the profit to be achieved.

- Defines a desired future business state which strongly draws people toward its achievement.

- Consistently operates from a strong and clear definition of the business outcomes he or she is trying to achieve.

- Successfully integrates an understanding of the dynamics of the business into a coherent business vision.

1	2	3	4	5	6	7	8	9
DEFICIENCY							STRENGTH	

REJECTION LETTER
(Interviewed; no interest)

September 10, 1996

Mr. Robert Tinnon
147 Maple Avenue
Topeka, Kansas 71894

Dear Mr. Tinnon:

Thank you for taking the time to meet with us last Thursday to discuss inventory control opportunities at Farraday Electronics.

We have carefully reviewed your background as it relates to this position. Although your overall background is good, there were other candidates whose experience was closer to our requirements.

We wish you the best of luck in your career explorations and express our sincere appreciation for your interest in Farraday Electronics.

Sincerely,

Joyce Cantrell
Recruitment Manager

JC:jap

OFFER LETTER
(Nonexempt staff employee)

February 14, 1997

Ms. Audrey Arbizanni
1006 Whitney Avenue
Far Hills, NJ 16904

Dear Audrey:

We are pleased to confirm our offer of employment to you as benefit analyst,
reporting to Joan Larson and starting March 1, 1997. We look forward to a
mutually rewarding relationship.

Your hourly rate will be $9.75. Your normal schedule will be a 38¾-hour week,
although some overtime may be required. You will be entitled to two weeks
vacation per year, prorated for employment of less than one year, to be taken at
times approved by your supervisor. In addition, you will be eligible to
participate in our fringe benefits program, as outlined in Attachment 1. The
various programs and their provisions will be reviewed with you upon formal
enrollment. These programs may be altered from time to time.

This offer is conditioned upon satisfactory review of your references, and your
ability to produce evidence of employment eligibility in the form of a birth
certificate, military record, passport or driver's license, along with a social
security card.

Please understand that nothing contained in this offer letter is intended to
create a contract of continued employment. Should you accept this or any other
position with our company, your employment shall be at-will and as such be
subject to termination, by either you or the company, at any time.

It is my hope that you will join us. Please complete the enclosed copy of this
letter and return it to my attention.

Very truly yours,

I confirm that I have read and understand the
terms and conditions stipulated in the above
offer of employment. I agree to accept these
terms of employment.

John Ellis, Jr.
Director of Administration

_____   _____
(signature)   (date)

OFFER LETTER
(Commission Sales Rep)

December 11, 1996

Mr. Richard Sauer
1441 Alabaster Avenue
Anchorage, Alaska 98411

Dear Richard:

I am pleased to offer you the position of sales representative in our Pacific Division.

Your salary will consist of a biweekly draw at the rate of $26,000 per year, plus earned commissions. Your commission plan will consist of ten percent of gross profit dollars generated, less the draw, payable monthly in arrears. Your commission will be guaranteed for the first ninety days at $960 per month. The compensation plans will be reviewed quarterly and may be adjusted to reflect your performance or current business conditions.

You will be provided the following relocation assistance:

— Packing and shipping of your household goods from Anchorage to Bellingham, Washington

— Final travel costs for your trip from Anchorage to Bellingham, in accordance with corporate policy

— One house-hunting trip of no more than three days in length to explore living accommodations in Bellingham, in accordance with corporate travel policy

— One month's rent in the new location.

It is my pleasure, Richard, to extend this offer. We wish you success in your new position. Kindly sign and return this letter to me if these terms are agreeable to you.

Sincerely,

Richard Sauer

Richard R. Farson
National Sales Director _____ _____

(signature)   (date)

OFFER LETTER
(Exempt Staff Manager)

May 21, 1997

Ms. Martha Dahlin
46 Sandholm Street
Geneva, IL 60134

Dear Martha:

Welcome to the Goodheart-Wilcox team! Writing this letter is a real pleasure for me. I look forward to working with you in your new role as Executive Editor of *Consumer Education*.

Martha, the following will summarize our employment offer and your subsequent acceptance:

1. Annual salary of $55,000, beginning June 15, 1997. Your first salary review will be June 15, 1998.

2. Participation in Goodheart-Wilcox's bonus plan. This plan is based on company achievement of 15% growth above prior year's bottom line. Your participation in the plan will be based on 10% of your annual salary.

3. Goodheart-Wilcox will pay for moving your family and household possessions from Geneva to Media, Pennsylvania.

   a. All your packing will be included on the front end of your move and unloading only on the back end.

   b. Your living expenses while working in Media will be paid by the company up to the time you move into your Media-area residence or for four months (beginning June 1997), whichever occurs first.

4. We will pay expenses incurred by you and your husband to return to Geneva for the closing of your Geneva residence.

Please sign one copy of this letter and return it to my attention. The second copy is for your files. I am delighted that you are now part of the Goodheart-Wilcox Company.

Most sincerely,   Signed and agreed to:

                                   Martha Dahlin

David C. Naden
Editorial Director   _____   _____
                                        (signature)   (date)
DCN:mab
Enclosure

NatWest Bank N.A.
SELECTION INTERVIEWING OUTLINE

1. Establish rapport
   - Greetings and introductions
   - Brief small talk

2. Set the stage
   - Why?—The purpose of the interview
   - What?—What will be covered
   - How?—The sequence of events

3. The Interview—Probe using open ended questions and the Interview and Selection Guide

   A. Discuss work experience—begin with earliest jobs and proceed to most recent position.
      Briefly discuss:
      - Duties and responsibilities
      - Skill and abilities
      - Public contact and service
      - Likes and dislikes
      - Difficult situations
      - Performance/Attendance record
      - Reason for leaving (probe deeply for data)

   B. Educational and outside experiences:
      - Grade average
      - Best and worst courses
      - Extracurricular activities
      - Team involvement and other outside experiences

   NOTE: Most of this work and educational information will be on the resume/application. Do not have the applicant repeat what is on the paper.

4. Discuss and evaluate key selection criteria
   - Customer service orientation
   - Honesty and integrity
   - Learning potential
   - Comfort with pressure
   - Team player
   - Detail oriented
   - Reliability and dependability
   - "Will Criteria" (What must be evaluated to "match" the candidate to the job).

5. Tell and sell
   - Explain bank and branch structure
   - Typical daily job duties
   - Branch relationships
   - Ask applicant if they have any questions or comments

6. Close interview
   - Tell applicant of next step—the recruiter will be in contact within a certain time frame. Thank the applicant for their time.

NatWest Bank N.A.'s
PERMISSIBLE INQUIRIES AND PROHIBITED
OR SUSPICIOUS INQUIRIES

Permissible Inquiries
- Appearance as related to job functions
- Authorization to work in United States
- Education
- Military work experience
- Past job experience

Prohibited or Suspicious Inquiries:
- Age
- Color
- Marital status
- National origin
- Physical/mental disability
- Race
- Religion
- Sex
- Arrest record
- Childcare problems
- Contraceptive practices
- Credit references
- Height and weight
- Plans to have children
- Transportation
- Type of discharge from service
- Unwed motherhood

GARTNER GROUP, INC. — POSITION OUTLINE

Position Title	Reports To (Position Title)
Organization/Department	Date Position To Be Filled By

1. **BASIC PURPOSE:** Briefly describe (in one or two sentences) the overall purpose or function of the position. Please note any unique aspect. If the position is an Executive Assistant, attach a plan for rotational assignments and a discussion of potential career path movement. _____

_____
_____
_____
_____
_____
_____

2. **PRINCIPAL ACCOUNTABILITIES:** Summarize the principal accountabilities of the position in four to eight brief statements in order of importance. _____

_____
_____
_____
_____
_____
_____
_____
_____
_____
_____
_____
_____
_____
_____
_____
_____
_____
_____
_____

POSITION REQUIREMENTS
QUALIFICATION CATEGORIES

Absolutely Necessary Qualifications—Those qualifications which constitute the minimum requirements for the position without which no candidate may be considered.

Desirable Qualifications—Those qualifications which improve ability to do the job and which indicate a preferred candidate.

EDUCATION:

Specify course of study, special programs and degree as necessary, such as MBA degree, graduate courses in marketing, courses in operations research, finance, etc.

Necessary _____

Desirable _____

KNOWLEDGE:

Indicate necessary general job knowledge, knowledge of factual data, method and processes and theoretical knowledge, such as knowledge of competitive market operations, technical products, computer programming, etc.

Necessary _____

Desirable _____

EXPERIENCE:

Indicate specific on-the-job experience necessary, such as experience in development of major contract proposals, in directing research projects, in consulting.

Necessary _____

Desirable _____

SPECIAL REQUIREMENTS:

Indicate special aptitudes and abilities necessary or desirable, such as writing ability, freedom to travel extensively, specialized outside contacts, etc.

Necessary _____

Desirable _____

RANK THE THREE MOST IMPORTANT REQUIREMENTS FOR THIS POSITION

_____

_____

COMMENTS: _____

_____

Prepared By	Date	Approved By	Date

Application To Join Our Team

Stew Leonard's®

100 Westport Avenue, Norwalk, CT 06851
(203) 847-7214

99 Federal Road, Danbury, CT 06811
(203) 790-8030

Today's Date:

Identification

Name _____ _____ _____
     LAST   FIRST   MIDDLE

Present Address _____ _____ _____ _____
                NUMBER   STREET   CITY   STATE   ZIP

SOCIAL SECURITY NO.

Tel. # _____ U.S. Citizen? ☐Yes ☐No Alien Card # _____ How Long? _____

Are you at least 16 years old? _____ Do you have working papers? _____ Exp. Date _____

Are you a veteran? _____ Branch of service _____ From _____ To _____

Have you ever been convicted of a crime other than a traffic violation? ☐Yes ☐No
If yes, please explain and give date, circumstances, nature and disposition of the case.

Employment Interest

☐ Norwalk   ☐ Danbury   ☐ Full Time   ☐ Part Time   ☐ Seasonal

Position applying for: *Please mark your first and second choice.*

☐ Meat ☐ Grocery ☐ Ice Cream ☐ Security ☐ Cashier
☐ Bakery ☐ Fish ☐ Produce ☐ Salad Bar ☐ Receiving
☐ Deli ☐ Office ☐ Barbecue ☐ Accounting ☐ Building Services
☐ Popcorn ☐ Customer Service ☐ Other _____

If you are applying for a management position, please attach resume.

Have you ever worked or applied for work here? ☐ Yes ☐ No

Worked☐Date (From)_____ (To)_____ Applied☐Date_____

What hours are you available? Please indicate days and hours.

Mon_____ Tues_____ Wed_____ Thur_____ Fri_____ Sat_____ Sun_____

Total number of hours willing to work a week _____ Date you can start work _____
Are you presently employed? ☐Yes ☐No

Referred by: ☐Advertising ☐Own Initiative ☐Stew Leonard's Team Member

Due to the nature of Stew Leonard's business, I understand that if I am hired, I may be required to
work nights, holidays, and weekends, and in various departments: _____ (Initials)
Would you be willing to work overtime? ☐Yes ☐No

Employment History

Even if you submit a resume, please list your work experience below, beginning with your present or most recent employer. Please include any summer, part-time or volunteer experience.

Present or Most Recent Employer		From Mo/Yr	To Mo/Yr	Job Title - Start
Address			Starting Salary/Wage per Week	Job Title - Present / Termination
City	State	Zip	$	Reason for Leaving or Wanting to Leave
Name of Immediate Supervisor		Telephone #	Present/Ending Salary/Wage per Week	Major Responsibilities
Title	Department		$	

Present or Most Recent Employer		From Mo/Yr	To Mo/Yr	Job Title - Start
Address			Starting Salary/Wage per Week	Job Title - Present / Termination
City	State	Zip	$	Reason for Leaving or Wanting to Leave
Name of Immediate Supervisor		Telephone #	Present/Ending Salary/Wage per Week	Major Responsibilities
Title	Department		$	

Present or Most Recent Employer		From Mo/Yr	To Mo/Yr	Job Title - Start
Address			Starting Salary/Wage per Week	Job Title - Present / Termination
			$	Reason for Leaving or Wanting to Leave
City	State	Zip	Present/Ending Salary/Wage per Week	Major Responsibilities
Name of Immediate Supervisor		Telephone #		
Title	Department		$	

Present or Most Recent Employer		From Mo/Yr	To Mo/Yr	Job Title - Start
Address			Starting Salary/Wage per Week	Job Title - Present / Termination
			$	Reason for Leaving or Wanting to Leave
City	State	Zip	Present/Ending Salary/Wage per Week	Major Responsibilities
Name of Immediate Supervisor		Telephone #		
Title	Department		$	

Present or Most Recent Employer		From Mo/Yr	To Mo/Yr	Job Title - Start
Address			Starting Salary/Wage per Week	Job Title - Present / Termination
			$	Reason for Leaving or Wanting to Leave
City	State	Zip	Present/Ending Salary/Wage per Week	Major Responsibilities
Name of Immediate Supervisor		Telephone #		
Title	Department		$	

Skills & Education

School	Name & Address of School	Course of Study	Check Last Year Completed				Did You Graduate	List Diploma or Degree
High			1	2	3	4	☐ Yes ☐ No	
College			1	2	3	4	☐ Yes ☐ No	
Other (Specify)			1	2	3	4	☐ Yes ☐ No	

Please indicate any skills or knowledge of equipment which you have been trained on. (Language, machinery or computers, etc.)

Extra-curricular activities (exclude racial, religious or nationality groups)

_____

Are you related to any Team Member currently working at Stew Leonard's? ☐ Yes ☐ No
If yes, whom: _____

Have you ever been discharged from a job other than a layoff? ☐ Yes ☐ No
If yes, please explain and identify the company. _____

_____

Why are you applying to Stew Leonard's? _____

_____

Please list 3 people that may be used for personal references who are not related to you.

Name	Occupation	Years Known	Address	Phone

TO BE READ AND SIGNED BY ALL APPLICANTS

It is Agreed and Understood That:

1. Completing this application will in no way assure that I will be employed.

2. This application was completed by me; all entries on it and information in it are true and complete to the best of my knowledge, and any misrepresentations of information given shall be considered an act of dishonesty. I understand that any falsification or misrepresentation herein could result in my discharge in the event I am employed by Stew Leonard's. I will furnish freely such information or documents that may be required to complete my employment file.

3. I hereby authorize Stew Leonard's or its agents to investigate my previous record of employment to ascertain any and all information which may concern my record, whether same is of record or not, and I release my former employer from all liability for any damage on account of furnishing such information.

4. If employed, I understand that such employment is subject to the Security and Bonding Policies of Stew Leonard's.

5. In the event of my leaving Stew Leonard's for any cause, I authorize Stew Leonard's to answer any and all inquiries as to my conduct and qualifications while working for the company, and cause of my leaving.

6. I understand that if I am a qualified candidate for a job opening, I will be required to successfully undergo a drug screening as a condition of my employment. The signing of this form is my permission for Stew Leonard's or its agent to take samples of my urine and perform a drug screening test on such samples. Further, I give my consent for the release of the test results to authorized company management for appropriate review.

7. I understand that if employed, the number of hours I work may fluctuate with business needs.

8. I understand that my employment with Stew Leonard's can be terminated with or without cause at any time at either my option or the company's option. No person employed by, or who is an agent of Stew Leonard's except Stew Leonard, Jr. has the authority to enter into any agreement, express or implied, for employment for any specified period of time.

Date _____ Applicant's Signature _____ Witness _____

DO NOT WRITE BELOW THIS LINE - FOR OFFICE USE ONLY

Interviewing Status:

Hired _____ Hold _____ No Interest _____

Hiring Status: Date _____ Dept. _____
Position _____ Orientation Date _____
Drug Test Date _____ Date of References _____
Interviewed By _____ Manager Interviewing _____

Schedule agreed upon by Applicant and Manager

Mon	Tues	Wed	Thur	Fri	Sat	Sun

Manager _____ Applicant _____

BACKGROUND INVESTIGATION RELEASE FORM

NAME (Print) _____

       (First)   (Middle)   (Last)

PRESENT ADDRESS _____   DATES

          (House #) (Street)   FROM/TO: _____ – _____

           _____

           (Town)   (State)   (Zip)

PLEASE LIST YOUR PREVIOUS ADDRESSES FOR THE PAST 7 YEARS

                                   DATES

1. _____   FROM/TO: _____ – _____

                                   DATES

2. _____   FROM/TO: _____ – _____

                                   DATES

3. _____   FROM/TO: _____ – _____

Date of Birth: _____

          (Month)   (Day)   (Year)

S.S.#:_____ – _____ – _____

Driver Lic.# _____   State _____

To assist in the evaluation of my employment qualifications, I hereby authorize Stew Leonard's, hereinafter to be referred to as COMPANY, and Danbee Investigations (their investigative representatives), to request and receive any information concerning me, including but not limited to, reports from any persons, schools, companies, corporations, partnerships, associations, credit bureaus, law enforcement agencies, licensing agencies, and any current or previous employers.

I authorize any of the above parties to furnish COMPANY, and/or Danbee Investigations, with any and all information concerning me, including but not limited to, credit reports. I further agree to release COMPANY, and Danbee Investigations, from any and all liability and responsibility arising out of the release of any such information or credit report.

Understood and agreed to by:

SIGNED:_____

DATED: _____

WITNESSED:_____

DANBEE
INVESTIGATIONS

INDEX

Achievement, 28
Answers, clarifying, 51–52
Application forms, 20–23
    sample, 112–119
Assessment, pre-employment,
    15–17

Behaviors, leadership, 7
Biases, 57
Bonuses, 72–74

Change, managing, 28, 31
Communications, 7
Compensation, 70–76
Computer aided recruitment, 15
Consultants, 17–18
Corporate mission, 4–8
Counteroffer, 75–76

Discrimination, 10–14
Diversity, 7

Empowerment, 7–8
Equal employment opportunity,
    10–14
Ethical behavior, 7
Exempt employees, 20
Exit interviews, 82–86

Functional resume, 22

Hiring:
    criteria, subjective, 16–17
    policy, 2–18
Honesty, 37–40

Information interviews, 89–90
Initiative, 28
Intelligence, 28
Interviews:
    computer aided, 36–37

ending, 52–53
evaluating, 56–67
exit, 82–86
guides, sample, 94–103
mistakes, 33–36
outline, sample, 108–109
performance evaluation, 78–82
preparation, 20–40
questions, 31–32, 42–45
    clarifying answers, 51–52
    initial, 48–49
rating systems, 58–60
selection, 42–53
structure, 27–29
termination, 86–89
Interviewers:
preparation, 23–25
style, 25–27

Job description, 9–10
    sample, 110–111

Leadership, 7–8, 29, 32

Mission, corporate, 4–8

Neatness, 22–23
Negotiation, 70–76
    bonuses, 72–74
    salary, 72–73
Non exempt employees, 20
Non-profit organizations, 4

Offer, 70–76
    letter, 76
        sample, 105–108

Performance evaluation, 78–82
    pitfalls, 81–82
    preparation, 79–80

Position description, 9–10
    sample, 110–111
Priorities, organizational, 2–18

Rating systems, 58–60
Recognition, 7
Recruitment, 14–15
    computer aided, 15
Reference checking, 64–67
Rejection letter, sample, 104
Release form, sample, 120
Resumes, 20–23
    functional, 22

Salary, 72–73
Self esteem, 28
Style, 28

Technical competence, 29
Termination interview, 86–89
    preparation, 87–88
Testing, pre-employment, 15–16
Tie breakers, 61

Value system, 27